DAWN O'PORTER

THIS OLD THING

HOT
KEY
BOOKS

THIS OLD THING

DAWN O'PORTER

CONTENTS

HOW IT STARTED FOR ME

Around twelve years ago, while cycling home after a day's work, a small clothes shop caught my eye. I dismounted, mesmerised by the window. I peered in. The dresses were old, nothing matched, the shop was full, messy, cluttered. I chained my bike to a lamppost and went inside.

The smell was the first thing that struck me. It was musty, but not dirty. Old, but full of life. It smelled of the past. Like the pages of a book. I was surrounded by stories, each one hanging from a rail, waiting to be retold. The clothes spoke to me in a language that I completely understood. A language of fashion that I had never heard before.

Until this moment my relationship with clothes had been fraught. I loved them, but didn't understand them. I couldn't communicate who I was through the clothes that I wore, because I always got it wrong. But in this shop I knew instantly that vintage clothing was a way to show the world who I really was. And that is what clothes should do: they should be an expression of who you

are. So there I was, in a room full of ways for me to express myself to the world, and everything fell into place.

I tried on dresses that had lived more of a life than I had. Some had signs of wear, some were as good as new. Some told the tale of previous generations' political plights, and some predicted the future. The fabrics were beautiful, the prints were bold, and much of the stitching had been done by hand. There was more character in that little shop than in any book I have ever read. And the stories the dresses told would never have to end.

That was the day my vintage journey began. My relationship with clothes had changed forever.

VINTAGE
WHAT IS IT?

Technically, vintage clothes come from the 20s to the 70s. Anything before that is considered antique, and anything less than thirty years old is just second hand. However, I enjoy getting into heated debates about the 80s. We are just six years shy of the whole decade being technically vintage, and some fashion academics absolutely won't allow that it is. However, so many vintage shops stock 80s fashion, and it is so definitive as a style that I think it fully deserves its position on the vintage scale.

Personally, I love the 80s. I know you may have just recoiled in horror, and although I can't deny that some 80s fashion should never have happened to womankind, some of it is brilliant. Bold colours, strong shapes, loads of attitude . . . But while I don't want you all to freak out before we've even started, be prepared: the 80s are coming back.

VINTAGE
WHAT ISN'T IT?

Some people are put off vintage because they think it's people's second-hand tat that ends up in charity shops. But that's exactly what it's not. I love charity shops, but they're mostly full of stuff that people have chucked away rather than vintage. That isn't to say you won't find some real gems. Some charity shops (like Oxfam) do an edit, with specific rails for carefully selected items that do fall into the vintage bracket, but finding vintage beauties can be more luck than guarantee.

Don't rule out charity shops, though – apart from doing our bit to support the charities, when you realise how it makes you feel to discover something truly amazing, you will be dragging old ladies off the bus to get them to show you what they have hiding in their lofts.*

If you have always loved clothes, but never quite found a style that you love because the high street doesn't seem to notice how unique you are, then stick with me. This book could be the answer to all of your fashion problems. I will show you how to find a style that is right for you, where to buy it, how to make it fit you perfectly and how to stand out from the crowd in beautiful clothes that no one else will have. Sound good? OK, let's do it.

*Please be gentle with old ladies in your quest to look amazing.

BUY LESS, VALUE MORE

BRING THE ROMANCE BACK INTO YOUR WARDROBE – IT'S TIME TO START FALLING IN LOVE WITH YOUR CLOTHES.

'But I love the high street – it's so easy!'

I think the colour orange and tailored suiting are currently in fashion, but I don't really know. I gave up trying to keep up with trends ages ago. It cost me a fortune and I was never one for following the herd. Something about fashion always scared me a bit – I couldn't cope with the pressure of having to fit in. I now spend my money on things that I fall in love with, and because of that I always feel like myself and always have something I want to wear. It's a simple thing that should be obvious, but the truth is, so many people spend money on clothes they don't really love. And that only gets you in a tizz.

How many times a week do you scream at your wardrobe because you have so many clothes but nothing to wear? Before I discovered vintage, this was me all of the time. I'd have full-scale meltdowns every Saturday night. I'd pull everything out of my wardrobe like a rabid dog with its head down a rabbit hole. Then I'd sit on the mountain of clothes and stare at my pathetic face in the mirror sobbing the words, 'I have nothing to wear. And I'm broke because I spent all my money on crap I didn't love.' Sound familiar? Please say yes, or I just made myself sound like a right fruit loop.

The high street is all laid out for you. Your size is there, the colour you want won't be hard to find. You know what you're getting before you've even got there. Nothing wrong with that, but when was the last time you bought something that no one else had? That you couldn't wait to wear over and over again because you loved it so much for the way it made you feel? If the answer to that question is 'ages ago' or 'never' then trust me: I have the answer.

By changing the way you shop, the clothes you spend your money on will be worth every penny, and the pieces won't go to waste when the next season comes around. Vintage is timeless, and if you give it a go, you will rarely get bored of your clothes, and episodes like I described can be put to the back of the cupboard.

'But vintage will make me look old-fashioned!'

It isn't to say that because I love vintage I don't want to be current. One of the worst things you can do with clothes from another era is look like you are in fancy dress. The way to get it right is by mixing statement pieces in with your contemporary wardrobe, and not looking like you're trapped in a time warp. You can develop a style that means you can get away with anything. One day you can go punk, the next disco. You could have a Friday night out in a cute 60s baby doll, then shimmy Saturday night away like a flapper from the 20s. You could go to work in an 80s power dress, then have a quiet dinner with friends in a 50s circle skirt. Once you go vintage your choices become so much bigger. On the high street you are limited by what the catwalks are telling the shops to sell; in a vintage shop you have the choice of every era at your fingertips. A vintage life really is like a box of chocolates: you never know what you're going to get.

If you put the effort into what you buy, getting dressed and looking stylish is no effort at all. But the wrong shoes can ruin your good work instantly. I suggest investing in a pair of knee-length brown boots with a small heel, a pair of metallic ballet pumps and a pair of round-toe nude heels, not too high. It is almost impossible to find an outfit that won't go with one of those.

HOW I DO VINTAGE

Apart from the essentials – jeans, T-shirts, jumpers and other bits and bobs – I'd say my wardrobe is now about 90% vintage. I do shop on the high street, but it's not the first place I head when I want something new. I'm not suggesting you get this dramatic, but the change this has had on my self-confidence and sense of identity is immeasurable.

And I made myself a promise that I would only buy things I loved, and take my time and really think about what I was spending my money on.

I also decided to do most of my shopping in vintage shops, online and on eBay. Then I found a local tailor, who would end up becoming the second most important man to me after my husband (OK, that's a bit dramatic). I take my bargains to him and he makes them fit me perfectly. And no, this has rarely been more expensive than shopping on the high street, and all my clothes fit me just right, and I love them. But any price would be worth paying to not have any more Saturday-night meltdowns.

How to work with vintage

My way of dressing isn't about turning yourself into something that you are not. I will never advise you to wear Spanx, change your hair or wear shoes you don't feel comfortable in. Just develop an eye for spotting something that is right for you. But you do need to train yourself a bit if you are used to the way the high street is laid out: they do the hard work for you, and while that seems like a good thing, it actually makes it really hard to stand out from everyone else who takes the same easy option. With vintage, you need to be your own detective. All that's important is to find clothes that represent your true personality. So if your clothes are making you feel like the real you is hidden then what are you waiting for? Get hunting.

How to shop vintage

Something that puts people off vintage shopping is all of the rummaging it involves, and yes, there is more effort to put in than when you hit the high street. With vintage, you have to get involved. The shops are generally better organised than they might look, and most of them are full of carefully selected stock rather than the random jumble that vintagephobes (I promise I won't use that word again) seem to think. The good shop owners edit what they sell; they want you to buy things, so having a shop full of tat isn't in their best interest, is it?

As you sift through the rails, almost like a magic trick with a deck of cards, the clothes are turned over and turned over until you see the one you are looking for. And when you see it, you will know. Whether it's a colour, a shape or a print that catches your eye, always try it on. If it works, you will love it because you will feel like you discovered it, and that item of clothing will be in your wardrobe for keeps. Not tossed aside the following year when the high street is telling you that you have to start over again.

By shopping this way, you buy less and value more. It's a great way of building a wardrobe full of stuff you love.

By the end of this book I hope to have helped you feel emotional about clothes. It might sound silly now, but it is like falling in love when you discover the kinds of gems you will undoubtedly find if you give this a go. Vintage is about standing out for all the right reasons, and loving every second of it. It's fun, and I am going to teach you how.

HAUTE COUTURE

This dress was made from 300,000 pieces of glass by Charles Worth, the father of haute couture. He was the first ever designer to put his name inside a dress, the first to do a runway show.

It was made after the flapper period of the 20s, and was a bit more sexual, more body slimming than dresses of that style. It showed the form a bit more, and was once more floor length and formal.

The hot orange colour of this Pierre Cardin pure silk crêpe column dress was so on trend in 1967–8, as were the beads and crystals. Pierre Cardin was the great modernist of the 60s. His earlier work was futuristic, but this is now contemporary.

You will no doubt have heard of haute couture, but do you know exactly what it is? If I am honest, I didn't for years, even though I pretended that I did. 'Yar, totes, haute couture, I have loads of it.' Truth being, there is a good chance I will never have any. It costs more than a small island to buy, and is also incredibly rare. It's in the same category as collectable art, as that is exactly what it is: art.

The literal definition is high (haute) sewing (couture). It's the creating and selling of top-notch custom-made women's clothing. It's hand-stitched, no machine, and it shows off the highest skills of the artist who is, in this case, the designer. It really is the very top of the fashion world; nothing comes above haute couture. But not any old designer can create something magical and call it haute couture; the term is strictly protected for a very special few.

The design house must be a member of the Syndical Chamber of Haute Couture in Paris, and they must employ a minimum of fifteen people and present two collections a year, again in Paris. Each collection must contain at least thirty-five separates for day and evening wear. Pioneers of haute couture include the likes of Chanel, Lanvin, Pierre Cardin, Christian Dior and Balenciaga. A dress can cost anything up to £200,000 and can take between 100 and 400 hours to build. This is where designers experiment with new techniques to create truly one-in-a-million designs.

To give you an idea of how exclusive this is: there are currently only around 200 regular haute couture customers in the world. However, despite the small market, top designers continue to produce it for prestige and artistic purposes. It's fashion at the highest end, and a mere fantasy for the majority of us.

Couture

'Couture' without the 'haute' is also a term used for top-of-the-range, to-order clothing – but not to the level of intricacy and expense as haute couture. In the modern fashion world the word is used casually, but in the world of vintage, if something is 'couture', it will usually come at a price.

READY-TO-WEAR

'Ready-to-wear' is the English for 'prêt-à-porter', which is the same as 'off-the-peg'. It refers to clothes that are created by designers, produced en masse to standard sizing requirements and are literally 'ready to wear' by the consumer. Basically, it's anything that isn't couture, and ranges from the likes of Marc Jacobs and Victoria Beckham to what you buy on the high street.

It was Yves Saint Laurent who realised that high-end design houses could make a lot more money if they sold more accessible clothing than the usual couture, when he opened his prêt-à-porter store, Rive Gauche, in 1966. High-end fashion now had a little sister, and ready-to-wear would soon give birth to the high street as we know it.

DOES YOUR BUDGET WEIGH UP?

Do you waste money on clothes that you never wear? Now, I am no Carol Vorderman, but this is how to solve the problem the D O'P way:

1 Find last month's bank statement.

2 Add up everything you spent on clothes.

3 Gasp in horror and go and make a cup of tea.

4 Now go to your wardrobe and find all of those items. How many of them have you actually worn? And enjoyed?

5 Gasp in horror again, as you realise that you keep buying crap you never wear.

6 Now read this book from cover to cover and learn how to spend your money more wisely, and only buy clothes you adore.

7 Pour a glass of wine. Relax, it's going to be fine.

GET BRUTAL AND MAKE SPACE FOR THE GOOD STUFF

I've started to enjoy taking stuff to the charity shop. Not the physical journey, that's always a total pain in the arse – I use bin bags and nine times out of ten the bag rips and all the clothes fall out onto the street, and once I got a paper cut. That's right, a paper cut. From a bin bag that's not even made of paper. Anyway, the relief of getting home to more space in my wardrobe makes up for any stress or injury I acquire. And regular clear-outs of my wardrobe have stopped me buying endless amounts of crap that I will never wear.

THIS IS HOW YOU GET BRUTAL WITH YOUR WARDROBE:

1. Open up your wardrobe.

2. Take out the things you wear all the time. Put them in a pile (let's call it Gary).

3. Take out the things you love but haven't worn in ages. Put them on Gary.

4. Take out the things you like the idea of but have never worn. Put them in a separate pile. Let's call that Dave.

5. What's left in your wardrobe is what you chuck. Get them into a black sack and set to one side.

6. Go back to Dave, try on all the things you think you love but have never worn and make brutal decisions as to whether you keep them or not.

7. Be honest with yourself, and be realistic. Think why you haven't worn it and if that reason is likely to change or not. Maybe it has always been too small, the colour doesn't suit your skin tone or the fabric clings to the bits you hate.

8. Pop all your rejects into the bin bag and take it to the local charity shop.

9. Be careful of paper cuts.

10. You don't have to name the bin bag.

Note: Be sure to take notice of all the shapes, fabrics and styles you like and keep them in mind next time you go shopping. Don't try to duplicate what you already have – that will just make your wardrobe seem boring. Just know what works and what doesn't, so you don't end up filling your wardrobe with more stuff you will never wear.

That wasn't so hard, was it?

VINTAGE DECADES

I can't lie, it's the nostalgia that I love the most about vintage fashion. The fact that these clothes have weathered storms, seen social and political change and represented the position of women over the years gets me excited. It's fascinating to see the dramatic changes in how women were perceived – and therefore what they wore – from decade to decade. Such vast leaps in just a matter of years, from skirt length to the amount of flesh on display. Did you know that during the Second World War there was rationing on fabric as well as food? And who knew the female waistline had been through so much? Here, decade by decade, I talk you through the fashions that make them iconic and why they matter. I hope you enjoy reading this fashion history stuff, as it's the real reason I am so dotty about old clothes.

THE 20s

Our vintage story begins

Ahhhh, the Roaring Twenties. Possibly the most risqué of all the decades, and where the vintage story starts. The First World War had just ended and society was trying to forget its horror. There was a real sense of change, especially for women – they had just won the right to vote and with this newfound status they relished their freedom and partied like their lives depended on it. Optimism was rife, jazz was pouring out of the clubs and people embraced the fast life. A new breed of young woman was born.

Shimmy in . . . the flapper. Oh my, what a gal!

Known for being young and frivolous, the flapper was essentially a young girl who enjoyed a drink, loved to dance and allowed herself the pleasure of casual sex. Considered unladylike for her carefree ways, the flapper was rebellious to some, but she was just living the life she felt she deserved. The 20s were all about women giving a big 'up yours' to the system. Finally!

The word 'flapper' apparently comes from a northern English term describing young teenage girls. When a girl turned into a woman, she would dress with her hair pinned up neatly; until then she would wear her hair in a low plait that would flap on her back. Well, that's one theory . . . I have another. 'Flap' was also a slang word for prostitute, and I believe the name 'flapper' – excuse me for being cynical – came from society's non-acceptance of women behaving like men. How better to patronise their newfound freedom by categorising women as tarts? A hundred years later, I am not sure this issue is entirely resolved. But I shan't get into that now. Oooooh, but I want to. But I wont.*

*WOMEN WHO LIKE SEX ARE NOT SLAGS. Ahhhh, that's better.

Women's fashion in the 20s was a true representation of the times. What women had worn up until then we would now consider unwearable – and it was impossible to get into without assistance. Corsets made waistlines tiny and busts pronounced, and being female was more about the body than the brain.

In a bold reaction to the restrictions of heavily corseted gowns, androgyny became the look of the decade. Waistlines were set free in straight-cut tubular dresses, and camisoles flattened the chest a little. The female form was subtly hidden, but flesh was casually on display. The fashion was a statement that simply said: 'I might not be showing you the contours of my body, but I am still letting you know I'm here. Shall we dance? (Or just shag?)'

By the time the Charleston took over the dancefloors in the middle of the decade, ball gowns were almost extinct. This energetic routine was made possible by dresses that were much shorter and made of lighter fabric than ever before. Thin straps and slits up the sides of the dresses meant that arms could move and legs could kick out in all directions, and sequins and fringes added to this foray of motion to create as much drama as possible. The 20s were fast, fun and wild. A simple flick of a strap after a night of partying would have the dress on the floor . . . These women were *serious* about having fun.

The arrival of silent movies in the 20s saw the advent of media influence on fashion. For the first time people were looking to the stars for style ideas. Louise Brooks, undoubtedly the most iconic silent movie star of the era, inspired a generation with her style. She popularised the Eton Crop – a very short bob – which is now short-hand for 20s style. Media influence would only grow more powerful in the following decades.

Louise Brooks

Chanel 1926 LBD

With dropped waists and straight cuts, dress designs were simple, so accessories became key. Long strings of pearls (and now imitation pearls were available, so everyone could achieve the look), cloche hats and chiffon scarves were all ways to dress up or down. Women had options, and fashion became fun and exciting.

One of the most significant moments in fashion history happened in the 20s, and we have the genius that was Coco Chanel to thank for it.

When Gabrielle 'Coco' Chanel launched her Garçonne Collection, she revolutionised the way women would dress right up to today. The skirts were calf-length, with a controversial simplicity that didn't show off the female form but freed it up with a more masculine cut. Waistlines dropped to the hip, and her use of jersey fabrics, which until then had been largely regarded as substandard, allowed freedom of movement that, for the first time in history, allowed women to be – God forbid – comfortable in their own clothes.

In 1926 *Vogue* published a picture of one of Coco Chanel's creations: a little black dress, cut to the knee, straight, with very little detail. It was a dress for every woman, and the LBD remains a wardrobe staple to this day.

What the men wore

Suits were colourful but simple, with unpadded, slim-fitting jackets over trousers. For the guys, the go-to leg apparel was wide-legged trousers called Oxford bags, or plus fours. Both bow ties and knit ties became trendy, but the key daytime look was casual sportswear. And the trendsetter was the Prince of Wales, who favoured multicoloured golfing-style jumpers and trousers, and V-necks with white trousers. Tennis, anyone?

As the people of the 20s embraced a culture of decadence, glamour and parties, little did they know that the shit was about to hit the fan. The Wall Street Crash in 1929 turned the lights off on the party and ushered in much more demure behaviour and dress. As morale went back down, so did the hemlines. The Roaring Twenties were over.

THE 30s

The 30s was a decade rife with contradiction. There was the dark shadow of the Great Depression, with its high unemployment and economic misery, eventually culminating in the start of a world war. Yet there was also the growth of aspirational temptation, and women were the primary dreamers.

It was an optimistic era despite the hard times. People fantasised about creating lives for themselves that were beyond what they could achieve in the grim realities of the time.

Escapism was a favourite pastime, with Hollywood one of the decade's strongest influences. Unlike the silent movies of the 20s, the 30s saw the advent of the Talkies, which made cinema even more appealing. People flocked to the picture houses to be wowed by the stars, and costume departments became the guiding light for the fashion industry. This focus on Hollywood styles, coupled with the unaffordability of imported European clothes in the Depression, gave the American manufacturing industry the lead for the very first time. The Paris fashion houses were no longer the epicentre of the world's fashion industry.

In the 30s retailers cottoned on to the idea of influence, and the desire for women to look like their idols. Famously, a dress designed for Joan Crawford by Gilbert Adrian for her 1932 movie *Letty Lynton* was copied by Macy's, and reportedly over 500,000 dresses were sold.

Women's magazines also became big business. They were full of advertisements for products, from cosmetics to furniture, helping people dream of the lives they wanted to create. Aspirational products were dazzling the masses.

Joan Crawford in *Letty Lynton*

VOTRE BEAUTÉ

4 frs.

SEPTEMBRE 1934
23ᵉ ANNÉE - N° 295
PUBLICATION MENSUELLE

MODÈLE DE VIONNET
PHOTO MEERSON

Soyez belle, on vous épie...

The 30s look was very feminine – a large leap away from the androgyny of the 20s. Skirt lengths dropped down from the knee, back to the ankle. The silhouette was slender and elegant, and the waist was defined once more. During the day it was wool suits with shoulder pads and long flute skirts. By night it was long, simple gowns. Satin was a popular fabric and slinky low backs were the height of the trend. Women kept warm with fur muffs and stoles, hats and gloves.

I love a muff.

One revelation of the decade was the bias cut, made famous by Madeleine Vionnet. Taking her inspiration from Ancient Greece, Vionnet discovered that fabric cut diagonally across the grain, rather than with it, could flow more freely, enhancing natural curves. This offered women a very soft, feminine style, which became synonymous with the decade. One design label that bases a vast majority of its designs on this method today is Ghost.

Another key designer from the 30s was Elsa Schiaparelli, an Italian who used clothes to express her wild imagination. Chanel, her archrival, once described her as 'that artist who makes clothes'. Her collections were bonkers, ridiculous and utterly brilliant. Schiaparelli paved the

way for designers teaming up with artists, as she did with surrealists such as Salvador Dalí, to create clothing that no one had ever seen before. Just look at her 'Tears' dress. She also introduced vibrant colours to the fashion world; her shocking pink meant that colour palettes everywhere became a lot more exciting.

Another key look for the 30s was Art Deco, the design movement inspired by an exhibition in Paris in 1925 called the International Exposition of Modern Decorative and Industrial Arts (although it sounds a lot better in French). It presented an avant-garde approach to architecture, which by the mid-30s had filtered heavily into home furnishings and fashion. Hence the 'Deco' part of the name. It was modern, and used symmetrical composition and geometric shapes.

This decade was also the advent of man-made fabrics. Rayon, which dyed well and looked and felt like silk, became a cheaper alternative and made fashion more accessible. And bright Bakelite bangles became a popular alternative to precious metals, so all women could add a touch of glamour to their look.

Knitted suit

Schiaparelli 'Tears' dress

This yellow gown from the 30s costs £795 today. It's an unusual colour for the era. The criss-cross back shows off some flesh, while the extra material on the hips emphasises curves. The square neckline is characteristic of the 30s. This dress was completely handmade. It's sexy, but sophisticated and utterly divine.

Mae West

Personally, I wear very little 30s clothing, if any, but I still love this decade. I love it because of the attitude women had. Times were hard, and the flapper had gone away – possibly to return in a slightly different form forty years later – but the women of the 30s were still very sexy. The dresses were often sheer, body-skimming, revealing. This wasn't a decade for shying away, and I think the icons of the time had a lot to do with that.

Greta Garbo was one of the biggest Hollywood stars, but my favourite icons of the era are Mae West and the woman who was so exquisite she caused a king to abdicate: Wallis Simpson.

Mae West was, in my opinion, one of the funniest women to have ever lived. She went totally against the Hollywood grain (incidentally, she wore Schiaparelli dresses in most of her movie roles). Her firm looks and sturdy curves were a welcome sight for the everywoman. But what I love most about her is that she wrote a number of her own films, discovered the handsome hero that was Cary Grant and came out with crackers like: 'I do most of my writing in bed; everyone knows I do my best work there.'

The Duke and Duchess of Windsor on their wedding day

Mae was controversial. She said what she thought and she taught women that they could be as comfortable as men with being sexually predatory and confident. Mae was the Madonna of the 30s, minus the nipple petals. Schiaparelli's dresses were about individual personality, so it's no wonder they were a favourite of Mae's.

Wallis Simpson was the dark beauty who captured the world's attention when she mesmerised a king. When she married the abdicated King Edward VIII in 1937, she wore a floor-length gown designed by Mainbocher. Along with a matching long-sleeved jacket and gloves, the entire ensemble was designed in Wallis Blue, a colour developed to perfectly match her icy-blue eyes. This became one of the most copied dresses of all time. Known as the 'Wally', it was available in shops just weeks after the wedding.

One major advance of the 30s was the invention of the tampon. Not a fashion piece in itself, but it revolutionised swimwear design, meaning it could be far more flattering, feminine and fun. The days of 'sanitary napkins' were over. (Crikey.)

A cute 30s day dress

This taffeta material has a slight sheen. The long length is conservative, but the slight waist adds some interest. I love the button and collar detail. The shape is definitely moving towards that of the 40s, so I would guess this was from the end of the decade.

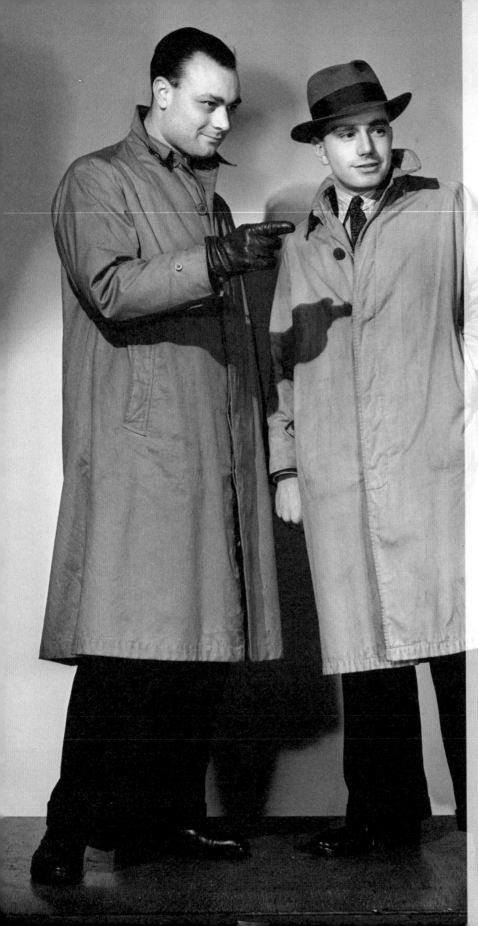

What the men wore

The colours worn by men in the 30s were mostly browns and greys. Preferred fabrics were linens, wool, flannel and tweeds, and lapels were often very wide and collars long, with button fastenings as popular details. In the latter part of the decade, jackets had taller sleeves and padded shoulders. Older men's trousers were tapered, but young men wore more long coats over wide-legged styles. This decade saw the introduction of the zip, a revolution in men's tailoring. All they had to do now was remember to do it up.

As beautiful and sassy as the 30s were, times were about to change for the worse again. When Germany invaded Poland in 1939 and the Second World War began, women's role in society changed again. They had to get to work – and they couldn't do that in a long, tight skirt, could they?

THE 40s

Military glamour

Please read the following in a wartime BBC announcer's voice.

The 40s were dominated by war. Even after the Second World War ended in 1945, its economic effects were felt well into the later part of the decade. People were nervous of indulgence, and shock waves from the atrocities had a sobering impact on morale. The war had blown the idea of extravagance up into the air, and the fashion industry took a massive hit.

Fabrics were rationed, as supplies were needed for the war effort. Skirts were to be at regulation length, on the knee, and they could only have a certain number of pleats. Pockets were to be purposeful, not for decoration, and even buttons were limited to essential use only. Looking pretty was no excuse for those kinds of details. Clothes that met all of these austerity regulations were marked with the CC41 'Civilian Clothing' label, to show that they had been made under the government-ratified utility scheme. The use of metals in clothing was limited, which took corsets out of the picture (thankfully). Nylon and wool were required for uniforms, so rayon and viscose became popular fabrics, as they were cheap and more readily available.

Clothes were bought with a combination of money and government-issued coupons. They were priced in pounds and coupon points, depending on how much fabric was used and how much detail there was in the designs. This was to encourage people to buy less and repair what they already had. The theme of the decade was

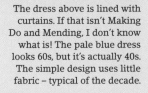

The dress above is lined with curtains. If that isn't Making Do and Mending, I don't know what is! The pale blue dress looks 60s, but it's actually 40s. The simple design uses little fabric – typical of the decade.

Make Do and Mend, a movement introduced by the Government to encourage people to restore old clothes rather than buy new, and where possible to make do with what they already had.

Women's magazines offered money-saving tips on how to sew, make and mend clothing, and use coupons effectively. Women with children were offered more coupons, but apart from that, you got what you got. The rest depended on how rich you were.

Hollywood was still hugely aspirational, with the movie industry reaching its highest ratings to date. Films such as *It's A Wonderful Life*, *Meet Me in St Louis*, *Gilda*, *Casablanca* and *Rebecca* were all massive hits, but the surprising top-grossing film of the decade was *Bambi*. Luckily though, Bambi wasn't considered a style icon. A pronounced hoof is never a good look.

One of the most influential movie icons of the decade, Katharine Hepburn, helped to make trousers acceptable for women to wear, often elegantly donning them in her movies and as she ambled casually around set. She famously said: 'I realised long ago that skirts are hopeless. Anytime I hear a man say he prefers a woman in a skirt, I say: "Try one. Try a skirt." It's hard to believe that it was only seventy years ago that women started wearing trousers without being seen as unladylike. We've come a long way!

The 40s saw the rise of the pin-up. Sexy, sultry, suggestive posters of high-profile women were sent out to boost the morale of the troops. One of the most iconic was undoubtedly Rita Hayworth for her role as the ultimate femme fatale in *Gilda*. This all blew up in her face, as it were, when the name 'Gilda' was inscribed on the Bikini Atoll atom bomb, as a nod to her 'bombshell' status. Reportedly, Rita was horrified by this, and very publicly made it clear she had no desire to be associated with nuclear activity. Fair enough.

Incidentally, if you like trivia, the bikini was named after the Bikini Atoll islands, where bombs were being tested.

Utilitarian-style clothing inspired by uniforms was the common look. As the men went off to war, women were thrust into the workplace. And as skirts were impractical for factory and other physical work, trousers – largely seen as unfeminine until now – were a welcome addition to female attire. They were high-waisted, typically with buttons down one side and a very wide leg.

For work, women needed to be practical and wear clothing that wouldn't catch in machinery, so dungarees and siren suits (an easy-to-get-into jumpsuit in case the sirens went off) were staples for all. Standard outerwear was trench coats and fur.

Military chic

There wasn't much to the colour palette of the 40s. Clothes were generally dark in tone, and there were lots of greys and dark greens too. But patriotic colours like blue and red were very popular, and a lick of red lipstick became the key ingredient to add a bit of instant glam to the more sombre shades of the clothing.

Typical 40s daywear for women was a military-style suit, buttoned down the front with a belted waist. The shape was boxy, masculine and practical. Pads (and you thought they were 80s) were used to accentuate the shoulders and give a more masculine shape. Shirt dresses were very popular; simple button-down fronts and a slim pencil or A-line skirt. Separates, when mixed and matched, were a cheap way to give the impression of more outfits. The 40s

are why so many of our grandparents and great-grandparents are frugal. They were trained to make the most of what they had.

Pussy-bow blouses were very common in the 40s, although they were first seen in the 30s and also associated with the 60s and 70s. Oddly, sequins and beads were never rationed, so although many evening dresses were simple and short, women would sew on a touch of bling to jazz them up a bit.

One other revelation of the decade, and another result of fabric rationing, was the bikini. Gorgeous high-waisted, low-cut bottoms with halter-neck tops that offered a perfectly pointed boob. Still, in my opinion, the most flattering bikini shape of all time. Grab yourself one – vintage shops are full of them.

One of the most significant moments in fashion history occurred just two years after the war ended, when fabric rationing was still in place in the UK. In 1947 Christian Dior launched his first collection, dubbed the New Look. Highly controversial for its dismissal of the regulations and its flamboyant use of fabric, some people found Dior's New Look very disrespectful.

The look consisted of soft, round shoulders, a cinched-in waist and a very full skirt. It was opulent and indulgent and a direct reaction to the fashion famine that the world had just experienced. Compared to the average wartime dress being made of a mere three yards of fabric, Dior's skirts boasted a minimum of twenty-five. The illusion of a corset meant that the female form was back on display. It's possibly no coincidence that when the men came back from war, women's curves reappeared too. Was this one of fashion's least feminist moments since the early part of the century? Possibly, yes. However, it was a welcome relief to a lot of women, who revelled in the joy of clothes being fun again. Colours and florals were right on trend. The clothing, and the future, looked bright once more. Dior's New Look would continue to be prominent into the next decade.

This grey suit was bought in Birmingham. It is dated 1949, so it's post-war. It was bought, not handmade. It is clear it's post-war because there is more fabric in the suit. The skirt is slightly longer than usual and has pleats – restrictions in fabric were easing off. The suit is very nipped-in at the waist and therefore has an influence of Dior's New Look. Women started to wear corsets again after the war, and clothing designs accentuated this silhouette.

What the men wore

Men in the 40s loved hats, particularly the fedora and trilby. Suits were generally slim-fitting and single-breasted, but for casual dress, men typically wore slim-leg, front-pleat trousers, a woollen jumper over a white shirt with cufflinks and a rayon tie, and brogues. Cardigans were popular, as were Hawaiian shirts. But really, for the majority of this decade, men were in military uniform. Though I am sure that didn't stay on long when they went on leave. *awkward cough*

So all seemed well, to an extent. But as the men returned home, the dynamic shifted dramatically. Women got out of the workplace and back into the kitchen. The war was over, and the wife was back.

And that was Dawn O'Porter reporting on the 1940s for the BBC. Goodnight!

THE 50s

The wives and the sirens

So the war was over and the men were home. It was time for the women to take a back seat again and for the men to return to work. Her job was to reward the man for all his hard work, and cook, clean, look after the children and pretty much just do what she could to make her man's life as easy as possible while he went out to earn cash. She played hostess for her professional husband. There were dinner parties, where she'd pull out all the stops to get him that promotion. The dresses were sexy enough that when she leaned over the table to serve the potatoes there was something to look at, but not so sexy that anyone got carried away. Yes, her role was to serve the men. How kind.

Of course, this wasn't her choice. *cough* feminism *cough*. The women who did remain at work were usually thought of as not being able to find husbands. And not being able to find a husband in the 50s was the ultimate failure. Women were either waiting on their men at home, or waiting to be swept off their feet. Either way, a woman's success was defined by marriage. How unthinkably depressing that must have been if you didn't fancy anyone.

As the world pulled itself back together after the war, there were more work opportunities. Young people had jobs and earned pocket money, so there was a bit of disposable income, and the fashion industry jumped at the chance to take it.

There was an emphasis on women being flawless. Etiquette, beauty and charm were all heavily marketed, and the media was full of products to help women achieve the ultimate state of perfection both at home and personally. Advertisements for cleaning products, make-up and furniture were all directed at women. Consumerism was taking off in a mega way.

A typical 50s advert for being a wife

Dinner, dear ...?

I'm just here to serve

Two typical 50s dresses: cute, colourful, girly. Small waists, big skirts and lots of polka dots.

Advances in mass production meant that ready-to-wear clothing became easily available. Manufacturers copied the haute couture styles in cheaper fabrics and sold huge quantities. Nylon was no longer needed for war materials, so that went back into making hosiery. Man-made fabrics such as rayon, polyester and Lycra, which didn't wrinkle, became firm favourites with housewives whose chore lists were already pretty high.

My favourite skirts of all time

Dior's New Look was the inspiration for most of the fashions in the early part of the decade. The very full skirt and tiny waist became the dominant shape for women. Sorbet-coloured cardigans with embellishments like pearls and beads were all the rage. Hair was either tied up with a ribbon in a casual daytime ponytail, or in loose curls for a sophisticated look.

The explosion of rock and roll after the film (and song) *Rock Around the Clock* came out in 1956 meant that, when they went dancing, girls needed dresses that wouldn't split when their boyfriends picked them up and spun them around, so full skirts in printed cotton became popular. Patterns included florals, checks and polka dots with motifs sewn on. My favourite was the poodle skirt – a circle skirt with a poodle on it: simple. Circle skirts are literally a huge circle of material with a hole cut out of the middle, usually worn with a petticoat underneath to keep it nice and full. Teamed up with a short-sleeved shirt, a ponytail and a neck scarf, this style is the epitome of 50s fashion. The look was youthful, and a massive leap from the darker colours and basic designs of the 40s.

Rock Around the Clock - classic!

Trousers, now largely acceptable for women, generally fastened at the side to flatten the tummy. They were high-waisted and worn with short-sleeved shirts tucked in. Pedal-pusher trousers (just below the knee) and capri pants (down to the ankle) were the most popular styles. Knits were also popular.

Doris Day encapsulated the girl-next-door look, and her influence spread far. It was sweet, cutesy and girly, in pastel colours and flirty styles.

Then there was the small matter of Marilyn Monroe.

Marilyn took the good, devoted, submissive wifey image, screwed it up and pelted it into the air using her boobs as the springboard, when she posed nude for the first issue of *Playboy* in 1953. Whether her doing this was a good thing or not is debatable, but at least women were no longer considered so one-dimensional – perhaps

The girl next door, Doris Day

three-dimensional in Marilyn's case. This was a wild alternative to the general attitude of the decade, and although most women were tied to the kitchen sink, some dreamed of who they could be beyond the home. This inspired a fight for freedom, but also a new style of skirt. The wiggle arrived on the scene, and the hourglass figure took centre stage.

Marilyn executed the wiggle to perfection in the red dress she wore in the film *Niagara* (1953). Women watched and learned, and bottoms everywhere were soon to follow in Marilyn's footsteps. What with that and bleaching their hair to echo her platinum blonde locks, 50s women were divided into two types: the wives and the sirens. There was a sense of expression, but limited freedoms. What they needed was a revolution. What they needed . . . was the 60s.

Grease

Although a film from the 70s, *Grease* is the perfect showcase of youthful 50s fashions. The girls danced in huge skirts, but played it cool at the diner in pedal pushers and pumps. There was lots of colour, lots of fun and it's clear to see how young girls were starting, or at least trying, to express their individuality in what they wore.

Brigitte Bardot

A key sex symbol of the 50s and 60s. She starred in *And God Created Woman* (1956), in which she played a sexually liberated woman in St Tropez. The film was a hit, probably due to the daring nudity and the fact that Brigitte Bardot is quite possibly the hottest woman ever to have walked the earth.

What the men wore

The 50s was the era of many looks, one being the Teddy Boy in his drape jacket with a velvet trim and high-waisted drainpipe trousers. For the older gents, double-breasted suits were worn with trench coats. Wool was the most popular fabric – for jumpers, ties, waistcoats and trousers. Younger men made wearing suits fun with a stand-out hand-painted silk tie in a fun pattern. But my favourite 50s look for the boys was the leather jacket and denim jeans. Think James Dean – the popular male icon of the decade. Now excuse me while I have a James Dean moment . . .

Oh bite the weenie, Riz!

Brigitte, looking pretty secure in the fact that she is perfect

Trying to get my husband to do this hair . . . I'll keep you posted

Put it away, James

THE 60s

Freedom and the future

Ahhhhh, the Swinging Sixties.
Excuse me while I collect
myself for a minute, for
when I think of the 60s
I am filled with such a
deep, deep sadness that I
wasn't there. Oh to wake up
from a drug-induced sleep
head to toe in Pierre Cardin,
my eyes thick with liner, my
bouffant flopped to one side, having
danced like a lunatic to The Beatles all
night while revelling
in my newfound freedoms.
Alas, I can never go
back, so I shall
continue
to drown
myself in
fashions
from the
decade in an attempt to
understand how it might have felt to
be in the midst of the revolution that was
this incredible era.

The introduction of the contraceptive pill in 1961 brought
a sense of freedom that was to change women forever.
Finally in control of their own bodies and futures, they
were confident and determined to step onwards. Women
went back into the work place and, sure, most roles were
support roles – as secretaries to the big boys (see *Mad
Men*) – but what matter? They were moving forward.
Women had money of their own to spend on clothes,
they were getting out of the kitchen and finding ways

Don't lose your hat!

to be independent. Morale was high, and so were the hemlines.

The waist disappeared again in the 60s and the shift dress became the iconic shape of the decade. A shift is pretty much any dress that doesn't have a fitted waist. It allows a woman to be unrestricted and to move freely. Funny, isn't it? How the shape of a dress so blatantly represented where women were at politically. Remember how I said those flapper girls from the 20s were going to come back? Well, here they are again, but this time they're not going to be put back in their box.

Fashion started looking to the future instead of the past, and advances at NASA encouraged the couturiers of Paris – such as Pierre Cardin, Paco Rabanne and Rudi Gernreich – to create futuristic designs. But most notable was André Courrèges (possibly my favourite designer of all time), who created the mod (modern) look in a collection called Moon Girl in 1964. The strong lines, thick fabric and A-line shape were his trademark. He brought skirts above the knee and is often credited with inventing the miniskirt. White and silver were common colours, as he took his inspiration from the place that no man had ever been before: space.

Paco Rabanne was known for his dresses being completely impractical and largely unwearable – perfect for sexy super-woman Barbarella on a mission to find a missing scientist in space, though!

An André Courrèges beauty

Jane Fonda in *Barbarella*

The vast numbers of baby boomers born after the war meant that the 60s was all about the Youthquake. Teenagers swarmed the streets, music was influencing fashion and for the first time teenage girls didn't have to look like younger versions of their mothers. Fashion was targeted directly at the youth – because there were so many of them. Designers and production houses were copying the work of the couture houses and Hollywood costume departments, and selling it to the masses through ultra-fashionable boutiques in London.

Our beautiful capital was the epicentre of style at the time, with *Time* magazine first coining the phrase 'Swinging London' in an article in 1966.

The signature 60s party look was go-go boots, tiny skirts, pop-art dresses and clingy knits. It was the ultimate free-spirited fashion. Colour schemes were wild and detailed. Anything from huge orange flowers on a brown background to psychedelic swirls that created optical illusions. Monochrome prints were also very popular, and after Jackie Kennedy wore her leopard-print coat designed for her by Oleg Cassini in 1961, animal prints became a firm staple in any fashion-conscious woman's wardrobe.

However, the vibrant youth needed their clothes to be affordable, and it was our very own Mary Quant who took the miniskirt to the masses

Mary Quant trouser suit

(apparently she named it the 'mini' after the car she drove). Her look was high fashion, but with slightly more achievable prices, and the girls who bought her clothes were the mods that defined the era.

The prices at Barbara Hulanicki's boutique Biba were more affordable than Quant's (although still not cheap in the way that we think of H&M/Primark as cheap). Her colour palette was also revolutionary – using sludgy colours for clothes and make-up that hadn't been used before. Man-made fabrics were now fully commonplace, with nylon, polyester and acrylic being most popular. They were cheap, washed well and dried quickly. Perfect for the faster pace of life.

Arguably the most notable shape of the 60s was the A-line. A straight shape that goes from the armpit down to mid-thigh, or from the hip if it's a skirt. It's more rigid and symmetrical than the standard skirt and creates a very defined triangle shape. Until the mid-60s the waist was still a bit nipped-in, but as the decade went on the waistlines were let out.

Another very popular shape was the empire line – a cut that ignores the waist completely and falls from a seam just under the bust, and can be worn long

or short. This was a very popular shape for evening gowns, wedding dresses and maternity wear.

Of course, with a very short skirt, stockings were now an issue. Women couldn't walk around bare-legged in the winter or have their stockings on show, so tights (pantyhose) were popularised to solve the issue. Wardrobe malfunctions and corned-beef thighs in cold weather were a thing of the past. Here was another item that could be designed up to be fabulous, and Quant made them in fun colours and wild prints. It really was a decade where anything went. Colour, shape, print – and sex and drugs – were all to be experimented with.

By the 60s, fashion icons were just as likely to be models as Hollywood stars. No one was as desirable as Twiggy. This waif-like girl-next-door was the princess of mod. Cute as a button, with eyelashes thicker than her legs, Twiggy's image was, and remains, one of the most iconic of the era.

In 1966, Yves Saint Laurent was the first designer to launch a ready-to-wear collection. This meant the public could have an entirely new relationship with designers, and set up the 60s as the decade where fashion began to democratise. His Mondrian dress, a block-coloured tunic, was about the past, present and future. The fashion was dramatic and bold – how the women were feeling.

Towards the end of the 60s there was a return to a much softer silhouette after the stark lines of the space age. When Faye Dunaway appeared in *Bonnie and Clyde* in 1967, there was a move towards slinky midi skirts (mid-calf) and twin sets with berets replacing the pillbox hat that the likes of Jackie Kennedy had worn so elegantly.

You say Mondrian . . . I say L'Oréal

The hippy movement began around the summer of 1967 ('the Summer of Love') and its free-flowing social mindset was echoed in the fashion of the time. The dramatic lines of mod dresses were starting to become blurred; society was becoming more diversified. No longer could a decade offer just one domineering fashion; women needed more choice to represent who they were as individuals. Designers took note: the 70s was to be a decade of multiple scenes. As all those strong-minded, independent teenagers of the 60s merged into adulthood, it was time to give them what they wanted.

Jackie rocking a pillbox hat

What the men wore

Everything got longer and wider in the 60s: trousers, jackets, ties, lapels, belts . . . The mods were a big style influence. Mod-style suits were tailored, clean and form-fitting, and the colours were becoming a lot bolder. Mods were heavily influenced by the continent – Italian mohair suits and coffee bars, and French New Wave films – and they listened to cool jazz. Then there were the rockers, who were influenced by American styles and rock and roll. Outside these tribes, polo shirts were a casual look and, thanks to a group of four Liverpudlians and their album called *Sgt. Pepper's Lonely Hearts Club Band*, so was the Nehru jacket. (That's The Beatles, in case you are from the moon.)

Hello, boys!

THE 70s

Phew, no camel toe

Just casually waiting for a bus

Pick your tribe

When you think of the 70s, do you think of platform shoes and Afro wigs, or ABBA in their bell-bottomed jumpsuits? Or floaty, hippy maxi skirts? Or punk or glam rock? Point being, there were multiple popular looks that defined the 70s. It was a decade of variety that took inspiration from fashions of the past and created entirely new looks of its own. In short, from a fashion perspective, it was completely awesome. Let's break it down.

Hippy

The hippy scene continued into the early part of the decade, with long, floaty maxi dresses very popular. Designers were keen to get people wearing midi skirts (mid-calf), but the look didn't take off and had a pretty short shelf life. Dresses that skimmed the ankle – previously a look reserved for evening wear – were now worn casually during the day. This was a reaction to the geometry of the 60s. People wanted to feel relaxed. It would have been hard to dance around a field feeling free and full of love in the stiff, awkward style of a mod. Key designers for this look were Ossie Clarke and Laura Ashley.

Glam Rock

This was a post-hippy movement in the early 70s, with David Bowie and Mark Bolan as glam icons. The look was androgyny with a diamanté crust. It was rock and roll, but more camp, with more bling and wild hairstyles (see Bowie's red, spiky crop). Feather boas with Victorian-style shirts, painted faces, tight trousers with bell-bottoms and platform shoes. Subtle this was not. The music inspired it; the kids loved it. Shops that were acclaimed for the look were Biba and Granny Takes a Trip.

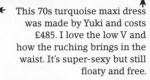

← This 70s turquoise maxi dress was made by Yuki and costs £485. I love the low V and how the ruching brings in the waist. It's super-sexy but still floaty and free.

←This maxi dress was made by Francar Doppiery. It is hippy and folky, with flared sleeves and a high waist. I love this shape, as even though there is loads of fabric it's still very flattering and gives you shape. A great one for big boobs.

← This is my kaftan-style 70s maxi dress. I love the shape of it AND the fact that it has owls on it. Owls, on my dress . . . this makes me so happy.

←In the 70s, paisley-print dresses – like this cotton one, made by Al Harbi – were massive. This one is also an example of a midi length. You need to be tall to pull it off.

Punk

Punk was a political movement: a reaction to the peace and love of the hippies that had now become mainstream. The UK's economy suffered terribly in the 70s and the depressed society inspired the punk revolution. When the Sex Pistols released *Anarchy in the UK*, punk fashion represented their anarchic attitude. Ripped jeans, torn T-shirts, safety pins for earrings, tartan bondage trousers, PVC, DM boots. The 'I put this together myself' look was key. To represent the times, the cheaper the look, the better. Key designers from this scene were Malcolm McLaren and Vivienne Westwood. When they started incorporating elements of fetish wear in their shop, Sex, it became *the* punk destination.

Disco

Studio 54 in New York was the most famous discotheque in the world. Luminaries such as Bianca Jagger (who rode through it on a white horse on her thirtieth birthday), Andy Warhol and Liza Minnelli frequented it. The outfits were extreme: hot pants, disco pants, halter-necks, zipped-up jumpsuits and platform shoes – all first seen in the 40s. Halston was the key designer for the disco age. Anyone who was anyone hung out in Studio 54, while the rest of the world watched on and copied the clothes and the moves. John Travolta's white suit was reportedly a firm favourite at proms and school dances. Imagine someone rocking up in that now? I imagine he would probably be dancing alone.

Whatever the tribe, generally there was a move towards ease and earthiness. Floppy-brimmed hats and brown knee-high boots were the accessories of the moment. In contrast to the space-age whites and silvers of the 60s, the 70s look was much more grounded. Leathers came as battered brown rather than white (or PVC), and the emphasis was more on easy-going than easy-access. Kaftans were hugely popular, as people looked to other cultural backgrounds for inspiration. Big lapels on shirts and jackets are one of the most identifying signs that these items are from the 70s, and are probably what people most associate with the decade.

Wide-legged jumpsuits and catsuits with bell-bottoms (thanks, ABBA) were standard party wear, and hair was worn long and loose, or waved and flicked into a Farrah Fawcett look.

By 1972 jeans were very much in fashion for women as well as men. And this was the first decade that saw the broad acceptance of trousers for women from start to finish. Finally, a woman could wear trousers without being thought uncouth. It's amazing it took this long, when trousers were first introduced to women by Chanel in the 20s.

Designers looked to the past for inspiration. Laura Ashley and Ossie Clark took their lead from the Victorian and Edwardian eras and designed granny dresses that had high necks and puffed long arms. This old-fashioned style was a vast contradiction to the drama of punk and glam rock, but that's what the 70s were about. Society was breaking off into sects, and the tribes needed to define themselves in what they wore.

Helen Reddy in a ruddy jumpsuit

This used to belong to Dorothy Squires, Roger Moore's first wife, and now it's MINE!

Man-made fabrics such as nylon and polyester were extremely common. Air transport became cheaper, so a huge range of fabrics could be used, and the large production houses were able to distribute their stock worldwide. Ready-to-wear became much more available.

The 70s saw the introduction of the care label in clothes. So this is a really simple way to date an item of vintage. If it doesn't have a care label, it could be a sign that it's pre-70s.

Missoni is an Italian textiles design house known for its distinctive patterns. The bohemian striped fabric remains totally identifiable as their own, even today.

The Queen of Knits, Sonia Rykiel was the first person to print words onto jumpers, and the first to put seams on the outside of clothes.

I saw this on a mannequin while filming *This Old Thing* and had to put it on.

French fashion model Amanda Lear in a new outfit by British designer Ossie Clark for Alice Pollock's Quorum boutique.

The other one is mine, gerroff!

Husband-and-wife team Ossie Clark and Celia Birtwell created clothes that were a favourite then and are highly collectable now. Celia designed the stunning prints that were used on so many of Ossie's stunning, flowing clothes, often made of wool crêpe. Ossie referred to himself as a 'master cutter'. I have to say, I totally agree. I am mad about his dresses and I find the idea of a husband and wife creating romantic dresses with beautiful prints on them quite mind-blowing.

What the men wore

Until the 70s men hadn't had much to play with, but now there was a big focus on colour and pattern. After John Travolta flicked his hips in *Saturday Night Fever*, three-piece disco suits in bold colours became huge (literally – those lapels were epic). The suits had wide collars and flared trousers, and the kipper tie succeeded the more classic shape. Other neckwear in the 70s included cravats and neck ties with flamboyant patterns. Belted trench coats were a popular choice of coat, as were velvet jackets, again with wide lapels, and tight-fitting shirts with low-slung pants. The fashion was fun, so the boys could just focus on staying alive. (That was terrible, sorry.)

Rod Stewart

THE 80s

The advent of contemporary dressing

A controversial decade in the world of vintage (remember, to officially be vintage something must be thirty years old), but one I defend. I was born in 1979, so my entire childhood was about this bizarre but brilliant decade. It's how I remember my mum and my aunties dressing; it's how I presumed I would look when I grew up. I was cool with it at the time, so I'm not going to abandon the idea now.

Though I have to admit, some of it was bloody hideous: enormous batwing jumpers, sequined dresses, peplum skirts, puffball skirts, shoulder pads like sunbeds, frills and ruffles, oversized everything and branding labelled on the outside rather than the inside of clothes. All together, a complete modern no-no, but when mixed in with more contemporary clothes, or even stuff from other decades, these statement pieces are really fun. Apart from the branding – that's always awful.

And I think you'd be surprised how much 80s-inspired stuff you have in your wardrobe without even realising. Peplum skirts, for example, have made a huge comeback in recent years. And don't tell me you don't own a pair of leggings. See? The 80s are everywhere. And while a lot of it should only come out for Halloween, many 80s trends bridged the gap between wild revolutionary fashion and a more contemporary way of dressing. It's true, hear me out.

The economic doldrums of the 70s continued into the early 80s, and many of the outrageous style tribes of the late 70s and early 80s – New Romantics, goths, from clubs like The Blitz – were a reaction to the expanding corporate sector, a celebration of the individual and of creativity. Then the 80s moved into a theme of excess. Where the partygoers of the 70s danced around in polyester trousers, the 80s saw the return of finer fabrics, like wool, silk and cotton, because people could afford them. As Michael Douglas said in *Wall Street*: 'Greed is good.' Branding plastered all over clothes was a symbol of what people could afford. The yuppie was rife, and to be a well-organised yuppie you needed the most valuable accessory of all, the Filofax. A revelation in its time, but nowhere near as good as iCal.

A key look for the 80s woman was power dressing. Some say – and I am sure they are right – that power dressing was a tactic devised to build women up in the workplace, to give them more authority. Sure, some women had positions of power, but the work environment was still very male. So, like a wildcat fluffing its fur to appear bigger to predators, the working girl of the 80s used fashion to warn her prey that she meant serious business.

And how did she do this? Suits became very popular with career girls, as did shirt dresses with suiting details. While short skirts were back with a vengeance, top halves got bigger and bigger. The bigger the better, in fact. Shoulder pads were the accessory of the era, often attached by Velcro so you could put in bigger ones if you wanted to (oooh, and plenty wanted to, all right). Shoulder pads have a terrible reputation, but they really are quite marvellous in moderation. Few women don't benefit from the subtle structure of a bit of shoulder padding. Big ones are hard to pull off, as it were. But there is no doubt that these acromion enhancers make you feel like you rule the roost, so it's perfectly understandable why this trend took over the decade. They filled women with the self-assurance to go get what they wanted. But which came first, the confidence or the shoulder pad? Well, that is one of life's big questions, and I guess we will never really know.

Designers like Katharine Hamnett were challenging mainstream ideologies, and also getting involved in environmental causes. Her T-shirts carried slogans like 'SAVE THE FUTURE', so people were expressing their political views before they even opened their mouths.

This makes my muscles ache just looking at it

An antithesis to the career girls were the New Romantics; evolved from punk, but interested not in austerity so much as wanting to party in nightclubs, adorned and glamorous. New Romantics took ideas from the waify 30s. Lots of eyeliner, with baggy, full-sleeved shirts and loose trousers with a tapered ankle. The finest example of this would probably be Adam Ant, but if you try to visualise Russell Brand dressed up as a pirate then you'd have a good idea of how this look was thrown together. Again, Vivienne Westwood was a key designer for this scene, working closely with musicians to set up an alternative style for the decade.

Leisurewear. For women, this meant the leotard. Mums everywhere were sweating into their headbands in the comfort of their own living rooms as aerobics and dance-themed TV shows tried to keep the nation fit. Olivia Newton-John sang about getting physical, and Jane Fonda was on a mission to give the world firmer thighs through the power of leg warmers and squat thrusts. The movie *Flashdance* made one-shouldered sloppy joe jumpers worn with a pair of leggings the must-have 'I'm cool' style.

My first true love, Madonna

Now, Madonna is possibly the main reason why I love the 80s. I was obsessed with her. I remember my mum telling me to stop singing about feeling like a virgin when I was no more than five. So I did it in the privacy of my own bedroom (I never saw the problem; I was one). I ripped holes in my clothes and I put my gran's leather gloves on as I screamed the lyrics to 'Lucky Star'. With skirts over leggings, fishnet gloves, Easter-egg bows in her hair and her bra on the outside ('by mistake', as my gran used to tell me), I was totally infatuated.

Madonna's style was a response to how women had been pinned down for too long. Madonna was telling us that androgyny shouldn't be the only answer to the equalisation of the sexes. She chose overt sexuality to *express herself* and show women everywhere how good it could feel to revel in the power of their own bodies. Madonna paved the way for a new kind of youth. A kind where women were on top. I am a child of the Madonna generation, and for that I thank the 80s for allowing someone like her to become the icon that she was and is.

The main thing that the 80s did do wrong was to ruin wedding dresses. Until Princess Diana blancmanged up the aisle in that puffed-up monstrosity, wedding dresses were elegant and demure. To this day women everywhere think they need to wear unflattering white ball gowns on the most important day of their lives, because of the 80s. And this, women everywhere, has to stop.

There, I said it.

Jeans were suddenly not just for work wear; they were highly desirable fashion statements. For the reason that they were expensive.

MTV launched in 1981, giving pop music a huge influence over fashion. Singers and bands could inspire entire fashion movements. Designers had to keep up with public demand, as fashion sped up in the 80s.

What the men wore

The 80s was a decade of showing your wealth, so men began to wear tighter, more close-fitting trousers (cheeky). Even casual wear and tracksuits were covered in branding to show people how much you had spent. Suits were single-breasted in blues and greys, with distinct buttons such as gold, and shirts had French cuffs (i.e. double-layered). The more casual suit was light linen, with pleated trousers, and more often than not worn with loafers and no socks. Shirts were in pastel colours, and men weren't shy of wearing pink.

The primary fashion accessory for men in the 80s was a moustache, inspired by *Magnum, P.I.*, and my dad.

OVER HERE, I'M OVER HERE

Arsenio Hall looking all casual and stuff

So what vintage works for your shape?

Think you are the wrong shape for vintage? I don't.

When you shop vintage, you are never restricted by what the high street is pumping out. Find a style that works for your shape and you can actively source interesting pieces from that era.

But where do you start? This guide should give you an idea of what to look for – but it shouldn't mean you cancel out styles from other eras. When vintage shopping, you must be open-minded.

Just try it on!

There is a common myth that women were all smaller or a different shape in the past, but that's mostly the underwear of the times creating a different silhouette. There have always been women of all shapes and sizes, so even though some decades have iconic looks that will suit you better than others, there is always a chance that you will find something wonderful from an era you wouldn't expect.

Use this guide as a starting point, but keep your eyes open for surprises. And remember, if there is something about an item of clothing that you love but you are not sure about the shape, just try it on anyway. There might be something a tailor can do to make it work. Just use your imagination.

Don't take any notice of the sizes on vintage labels. Over the years manufacturers have adjusted how they size clothing, and a size ten now, for example, is nothing like a size ten from fifty years ago. So don't be put off if you think it won't fit: always try it on. And if you are shopping online then make sure you know your measurements. Clothes are usually listed with their full details, so that's the best way to make sure you won't be disappointed. And remember, you can always get things adjusted.

If you find yourself falling into more than one of these categories, you probably already know what suits you. But as a piece of advice, don't waste your time panicking about the negative bits and stressing about how to hide them. Focus on your best bits, and dress them really well.

Are you an apple?

If you carry most of your weight around your middle, then you are an apple. I am an apple, so I know this one well, and the good news is that there are plenty of vintage styles that are great for you. I recommend heading for the 60s and 70s rails.

A shift dress from the 60s leaves the waist free, so it will skim over your tummy and you won't feel it clinging around your middle. A lot of people with an apple shape have great legs, as the weight has kindly deposited itself elsewhere, so take advantage and show off your pins.

Another great shape for you is something with an empire line. This is a loose-fitting dress that has no waist, but falls from a seam just below the bust. It draws the eye up, and gives the illusion of a long, slim waistline that elongates your body.

Depending on your height, you could work an empire line in both short and maxi lengths. If you are short, look for shorter dresses from the mid-60s; if you're taller, you can look for longer dresses, which come from the late 60s and early 70s.

Bold or optical prints will be a great distraction from your tummy. So have fun with the fabrics, particularly from the 60s, as that was an era all about vibrant patterns.

60s shift dress

Vikki Carr in a maxi dress, 1965

Are you a pear?

Pear-shaped gals hold weight around the hips and thighs. Is this you? OK, listen up.

Pretty much anything A-line will look great. This shape skims over your problem areas (what a horrible expression) so you will only have your best bits on display. Dresses are good, but a high-waisted A-line skirt with a cute top or a polo-neck tucked into it with a belt to nip you in even more would make this pear seriously delicious!

Another great look for you would be a 50s silhouette, with a defined waist and a very full skirt. You might also want to think about accentuating your shoulders to balance you out a bit – an 80s jacket with shoulder pads (size dependent on how brave you are) will widen your frame a little up top, but go for a cropped style so that it draws attention away from the hips.

Blouses with puffed sleeves are another good option. There are plenty from the 70s, when designers were looking back to the Victorian and Edwardian eras. Vintage Laura Ashley and Ossie Clark would be great places to start, although there are tons of cheaper copies out there to find.

Maxis from the late 60s and early 70s are great. If you have a narrow top, go for the summery styles with thin straps, or even strapless.

Are you top-heavy?

If you are big up top with broad shoulders or big boobs, then the 50s is your decade.

Avoid high necks or anything too angular. Soften your broad shoulders with a sweetheart neckline or, even better, a halter-neck. Halter-necks cut into the shoulder shape to suggest a more feminine curve, and also support the bust. (Think Marilyn in her

white dress – boobies perfectly in place.) A full skirt will also even out your shape and help divert attention downwards.

But if you don't want a full skirt, or too much flesh on display, a 40s tea dress is a great option. Simple, feminine and not clingy, so you won't be too T-shaped. Alternatively, try a 70s wrap dress. The diagonal lines it creates when it wraps give the illusion that you're narrower up top. If you can find an original Diane von Furstenberg (DVF) then fabulous.

Find dresses or skirts that have pattern detail around the hem to bring the focus down and balance you out. Vertical stripes are always a winner, but horizontal will make you look wider. Watch that your boobs don't cause the stripes to get bigger across your chest, though, as that will only attract attention to them. If that is what you want to avoid (boobs are awesome).

For an evening look, have fun with an 80s pencil dress with a peplum. Just be sure to take the shoulder pads out to avoid looking like Arnie in *The Terminator*.

Are you a skinny minnie?

Skinny Minnie? One word: flapper.

This look is all about cool, simple androgyny, and a slim figure like yours carries it off better than any other. Go for dresses with beads and sequins to add texture if you are worried about looking shapeless, then go get your shimmy on.

If you want to be slightly more sexy and sophisticated, look to the bias-cut gowns of the 30s. The fabrics were often sheer and unforgiving but would skim beautifully over your slim frame. Few people can pull off a slinky gown, so knock yourself out and show off your hip bones. That's what the 30s were all about.*

And if you want a more youthful and funky look, go forward in time to the 60s. Think Twiggy with her 'twiggy' legs sticking out of the bottom of those stark A-line dresses.

*The 30s were about a lot more than just hip bones.

Cute mint-green cardi

That's a silly way to sit on a chair

Twiggy looking, er, Twiggy

But if you do want to show off your straight-up-and-down-ness then how's about looking at disco fashion from the 70s? A one-shouldered leotard or catsuit would create a brilliant illusion of shape up top, without showing you as anything that you are not on your bottom half. Or maybe I'm just getting carried away. But if I was straight up and down, I like to think I would live in a catsuit.

I'd avoid huge patterns if there isn't much of you to carry them off (unless you see a pattern you LOVE, of course). Block colours and monochrome are best. So chic!

Are you petite?

If you are petite, avoid maxi dresses and long skirts, as they can very easily swamp you. Again, the flapper look from the 20s would work well. The dresses are short and you can wear them with your biggest heels. If you are feeling super-brave you could add a couple of feathers in your hair to make you look even taller.

Look to the late 50s and early 60s for a good hostess dress. The skirt lengths were creeping up from below the knee, and ideally yours would be just on it or slightly above. Find one that defines your waist and makes up for your lack of height by accentuating your curves. And, of course, wear heels as high as you are willing to go.

One brilliant vintage item for petite girls is a coat from the early 60s. Even though the coats are long, the sleeves were three-quarter-length and the features scaled down (small or no collar, simple lines, block colour). They are uber-chic and won't drown you with too much detail.

Are you very tall?

I am 5ft 9in and I'm always getting things taken up, so there is plenty of vintage for us lofty types.

I am not sure there is any style that doesn't work on tall people, actually. The world of vintage is your oyster. Beautiful long maxi dresses and short skirts from the 60s will work – but if you have a long body, the dresses might come up really short, so check the hems in the shop before you disregard them and see if there is anything that can be taken down.

You, too, can pull off the long, elegant bias-cut dresses from the 30s for a gorgeous evening look. But if you want something less figure-hugging, go have fun with the 70s. High-waisted bell-bottomed trousers look best of all on people with good height. A huge lapel on a blouse, dress or jacket won't take over your entire outfit if you are tall. Channel your inner hippy and enjoy the fact that clothing with big features, like a flare, a wild print or a massive collar, will all look great on you. Be careful with hipster trousers, though. I think they were the meanest thing ever to happen to women. They're adverts for love handles, no matter how slim you are. Personally, I think it's high-waisted all the way, especially if you are tall.

Also, you can totally pull off the midi skirt. It's a really tricky length on the wrong person, but that's not tall people. Vintage shops usually have plenty in stock. How about floaty, pretty florals for a day look; or a more 30s tubular shape for the office or going out? Lush!

Are you size 16 plus?

I am told constantly that vintage is for skinny minnies. Hear this: IT IS NOT TRUE.

You can't go wrong with a 40s tea dress. They are loose-fitting but feminine, so very flattering. They can be a bit boxy around the middle, so try one with a belt to bring you in a touch at the waist.

Trousers might be tricky, so I recommend you use the high street to find a modern pair of jeans that fit you perfectly, then mix it up with brilliant vintage tops, maybe focusing on the 80s for bold colours and prints.

Bobbie Gentry in a maxi dress

Three fabulous women

That looks heavy!

Hides all the right bits

Adele - lush!

flatter areas like your neckline or chest. Try a short (just over the bum) 60s shift with a decorated collar, tapered trousers and a low wedge heel for a classic daytime look.

Then for night there is the Little Black Dress. Black makes any dress even more flattering, but the vintage shapes are really fun. Take your pick from any era and find the LBD that works best for you, maybe starting with the early 60s. Enjoy this wardrobe staple, but in a style you would never find on the high street. Adele is a brilliant example of a woman with curves who pulls off the LBD flawlessly.

Be careful of maxi dresses, though. If they are too full then they will not flatter you, so choose quite slim-fitting ones. Again, crêpe is the perfect fabric for you. See Ossie Clark.

Jean Muir made beautiful clothes throughout the 60s out of jersey, crêpe, silk and cashmere. Her designs were cut perfectly and were about comfort and fluidity. You could look to her designs for inspiration, and keep your eye out for these fabrics: they fall over the body beautifully and would be very flattering for you. Sometimes her clothes pop up on eBay for reasonable(ish) prices. If you see one and can afford it, invest: it will be worth every penny.

Avoid anything too smocky, and don't hide under lots of material – it is rarely more flattering. Choose pieces with embellishments that

Are you an hourglass?

An hourglass figure means you have boobs and a bum that are in proportion, and a defined waist. Is that you? If it is, you lucked out: the 50s were basically dedicated to you.

So many body shapes are flattered by Dior's New Look, but for you, this style really is brilliant.

Nip that waist in as much as you can and let your boobs and bum do the talking. A full skirt might be your preference, but be careful it doesn't make you look frumpy. If the idea of a tighter fit, like a wiggle dress, terrifies you, please just do something for me: try one on. These dresses were designed to work with the female form, and the women who wear them best have the curves to fill them. Go for it.

But please wear the right underwear. I mean a bra that gives you good lift and knickers that don't give you a VPL. That isn't to say you should wear G-strings, because although this book is about the many joys of the decades gone by, 90s underwear was a terrible thing.

Also, you guys can have a go at the 30s bias-cut dresses. Though if your middle is very small, watch out for gaping at the back.

That doesn't look comfortable, Diana Dors

You can wear patterns, but you don't need to in terms of creating any kind of illusion. Why distract from the curves and shape you already have? Go for bold block colours and wiggle away!

Look up images from the eras I have suggested for your shape and get a picture in your head of how you could look. Even though I never want you to go vintage shopping with a specific outfit in mind, having an idea of iconic cuts and shapes will be really useful. And always ask the sales assistant or the shop owner what they have in the stock room – vintage shops usually have more treasures tucked away in another room. Just ask, and try everything on. And most importantly, have fun and be brave. Gwaarrn!!

85

THE HISTORY OF **THE MAXI DRESS**

The hippy look took centre stage in the summer of 1967, and counterculture grew over the following years.

Hippies were inspired by the political goings-on of the time. Their attire was free-flowing and colourful, representing an anti-war, peaceful and loving (also: stoned) state of mind.

Sorry, I shouldn't generalise. I'm sure not everyone was stoned. And every time your dad tells you he never did it, he is totally not lying.

Anyway ...

The 70s was the decade of the maxi dress – with a long, flowing skirt. In a reaction to the sexy, short, dramatic looks of the 60s miniskirt revolution, hems dropped from mid-thigh to ankle-length for a much more chilled, natural and earthy look.

Oscar de la Renta dressed Julie Christie in flowing maxi silhouettes in the 1965 movie *Doctor Zhivago*.

By January 1970 the Paris collections were working towards a longer dress shape. Yves Saint Laurent in particular was designing skirts that fell to the floor.

Designer champions of the maxi dress – Ossie Clark, Biba, Halston, Pierre Cardin – created elegant, ethereal shapes that embodied grace and femininity. Celia Birtwell's and Zandra Rhodes's prints were iconic of the decade.

I have a few dresses made by Ossie and Celia together and they are so magical. Nothing says the 70s to me like an Ossie and Celia creation. As the 80s set in, the maxi lost out to big shoulders and shorter skirts. But during the 90s, androgynous style became de rigueur and the maxi dress evolved into a casual chic look, loosely inspired by grunge.

The millennium saw another return of the maxi. Kate Moss was spotted in a very feminine tiered paisley number for a friend's wedding in Ibiza in 2006. Other celebrities were soon to follow and the maxi earned its place as one of the decade's most-loved skirts.

How to wear it

For an up-to-date look, wear a high-waisted maxi skirt with a knit polo-neck for the winter. Invest in some knee-length brown boots with a small heel. Throw on a wide-brimmed floppy hat if you're feeling brave; it really does finish the look perfectly.

For the summer, try a maxi dress with thin straps. Hunt for something without too much fabric, as many maxi dresses can be overpowering and make you look frumpy. Vintage shops are full of them, and because of the loose fitting and long length, this is a great thing to shop for online, as the measurements don't have to be exact and there is usually something a tailor can do to make it perfect for you. Wear with flip-flops for an easy and relaxed vibe. Then throw on some wedges for night-times. Personally, I love a maxi-length kaftan too. These are so easy to dress down or glam up, so keep your eyes open.

The 'bikini' – you know, a two-piece swimsuit – has only been around since 1946. However, rumour has it that it's been kicking about for thousands of years.

Let's head back to early civilisation. Taking evidence from Roman mosaics and murals, historians believe that the bikini was the swimwear of choice for the Roman woman. Then, at a time when cultural and moral norms were even more relaxed than today, the bikini was right at home. (They were a sexy lot!)

But with the more modest times that followed, it wasn't until 1946 that two French designers changed the way we dressed while frolicking by a pool. Jacques Heim, a Parisian fashion designer, first came up with a very revealing two-piece swimsuit. He debuted his creation in his Cannes beach shop in the early summer and named it the 'Atome' in honour of another recently discovered very small thing, the atom.

Atome - the world's first bikini.
It must have been quite a moment!

But it was French mechanical-engineer-turned-swimsuit-designer Louis Réard, shortly afterwards, who named the scanty two-piece the 'bikini'. He took the name from the Bikini Atoll, one of a series of islands in the South Pacific where new nuclear bombs were being tested that summer. Initially, he couldn't find anyone willing to model the bikini, so he had to hire a cabaret dancer called Micheline Bernardini to show it off.

A year later, in 1947, Réard's bikini was introduced to the mainstream US markets. Sales were initially slow and many Americans were shocked at its scandalously small size. It was even outlawed in some cities.

Brigitte Bardot wore a bikini during the 1953 Cannes Film Festival, which popularised not only the two-piece but also her home, Saint-Tropez, giving it the tag of the bikini capital of the world. Pin-up Hollywood icons such as Marilyn Monroe and Betty Grable also

used revealing swimwear as a career prop. Clever, really. And not so different now. See any lads' mag for details.

It was in the 60s that women really began to embrace the bikini. In 1962 it moved from being fodder for a *Playboy* cover (June) to providing one of the most iconic cinematic images of all time: Bond girl Ursula Andress emerging from the sea in a white bikini in *Dr No* (October). This was a defining moment of the Swinging Sixties, as previously too much of a woman's body on display had been deemed shocking.

From then on, the bikini became even skimpier. The string bikini was invented in the 70s, followed by the monokini, the tankini and the cut-out. Today, the bikini is by far the most popular swimwear. And think of the huge spin-off industries it has inspired, from tanning technology to the bikini wax. As the cut of the pants got higher, thigh brows became a thing of the past.

In the 50s the wiggle dress was the antithesis to Dior's New Look, and was as much about the boobs and bum as it was the waist.

Technically, the wiggle is a dress with a just-below-the-knee hem that is narrower than the hips, so you have to wiggle when you walk. Thus it is called the wiggle dress . . . Clever, huh? Say what you see, kids, say what you see. In this case: bum.

Very often there is a vent (technical term for a slit) in the back so that walking isn't physically impossible. Not to provide air to the thighs, although I am sure the fact that it also allowed more air up the skirt was never seen as a negative aspect.

The focus for many women at this time was on either finding or pleasing a husband, so wiggle dresses were a very popular way to show off one's figure without showing too much flesh. Perfect for flicking your hips from left to right to attract a potential suitor, and a sure-fire way to keep your husband interested.

The wiggle remained popular into the early 60s, often worn with a swing coat over the top. Some of my favourite images of vintage fashions are of women wearing just that, with one hand on the hip holding back the coat to reveal the dress, and the body, beneath it. I like to imagine they enter a room in the coat, then take it off with the words, 'Oh, by the way, I also have this!'

The wiggle disappeared for a bit, with versions in the 80s, but it's really the last decade where the wiggle's come back into the mainstream, being seen on the high street.

Good wiggle dresses are easier to find in vintage, to be honest. The impracticability of the skirt means that many designers now shy away from the old-fashioned design, in favour of a pencil cut. A pencil skirt goes straight down; a wiggle is tapered in. If you do find a wiggle, go for a darker colour – a deep berry shade, or a jewel colour – to keep it as flattering as possible. If buying online, make sure you check all the measurements and have a tailor on standby to fit it perfectly to your shape. The whole point is that it is figure-hugging, so get it as tight to your skin as possible. It's cheap to do, and you can choose how 'wiggle' you want to go. Note: some sellers get confused and market pencil dresses and skirts as wiggles: they are not.

How to wear it

The wiggle look is sexy, so have fun with it. Tall, pointy stilettos for night-time, a lower T-bar shoe for daytime. My advice would be to keep the make-up subtle to let the dress be the main attraction and avoid looking too pin-up. Find a swing coat that complements the colour and go channel your inner Marilyn. Go on, she's in there somewhere.

THE HISTORY OF FLARES

A flared trouser is any trouser with a wider leg width below the knee. 'Flare' could refer to the bell-bottom, wide leg, boot-cut, loon pant, elephant pant; so anything with a widened hem (or a silly name).

Bell-bottoms probably originated in US Navy uniforms way back in the early 1800s. The shape is functional for a sailor as they could remove their boots with ease, roll them up on deck or whip them off without too much fuss if they got wet. They were also said to help buoyancy; if floating in water, the ends could be tied in knots so the bell-bottomed bit could fill with air. But let's not put that theory to the test.

By the late 60s, the counterculture hippy movement, with its relaxed, laid-back 'yeah man' vibe, was on the rise. The youth were looking for a thriftier and more casual type of dressing, rejecting the straight-leg styles that represented 'the establishment'. As well as buying naval uniforms in surplus stores (ironic with the anti-war types), many hippies began to sew fabric into the outside seam below the knee to make a flared shape. I did this when I was a teenager. The needlework was shocking, but I sure felt cool.

Bell-bottoms in the late 60s and 70s were worn with Cuban-heeled shoes, clogs or Chelsea boots, and had an average hem circumference of eighteen inches – it would take one helluva cankle to fill that. And then later in the 70s loon pants (balloon pants) flared out even further from the knee to a whopping twenty-six inches. That was some serious flare action going on there.

The flare has seen a resurgence time and time again since then. First in the late 80s with the rise of acid house and the second summer of love. Then, in the 90s, the boot-cut leg was hugely popular – a refined version of the more crazy wide legs previously seen in the 60s and 70s. The boot-cut wasn't cut outwards from the knee; it had a more gentle flare over the ankle. The flare had another major moment in the early 00s when festival culture exploded, with its influences harking back to the music festivals of the 70s.

Today, wide-leg trousers are ever-present. Catwalks and celebs all show them off in varying forms, but perhaps not quite to the twenty-six-inch proportions of the 70s. And that probably isn't a terrible thing; it's a hard look to pull off. Easy to pull off physically, sure, but as a look? No.

How to wear them

Wear them with a fitted knitted jumper or polo-neck for casual but serious chic. Try it with a shirt or blouse either underneath or just on its own, tucked in or out. Accessorise with open-toe wedges, or just wear pumps if the flares are not too long. Add a fringed suede shoulder bag and oversized sunnies to top it off perfectly.

Try to incorporate different textures into the outfit. Leather boots with suede belts and hats will work a treat. Peace out.

Jane Birkin in Paris – was there ever anyone cooler?

At sea with the US Navy

Me trying to be Jane Birkin

The miniskirt is a small and sexy but highly significant piece of fabric. When it arrived in the 60s it denoted empowerment yet vulnerability, independence yet a desire to please; it covered yet revealed, was considered mature yet playful and emanated liberation yet exploitation. It was both condemned and loved.

The 60s were politically and culturally charged in general, but for women it saw the birth of modern feminism. In 1963 Betty Friedan published *The Feminine Mystique*, deconstructing the myth of the happy housewife and encouraging women to explore other roles. There was a huge increase in women attending university and entering the workforce in the 60s. Temp agencies began in this era, so women had greater flexibility in where they could work. Laws were passed to help protect and empower women through marriage and divorce. The pill removed fear of unwanted pregnancy and gave rise to the sexual revolution, with the miniskirt a leading tool of expression.

With so much change happening, the 60s became one of the most revolutionary eras yet, and the miniskirt was one of the major fashion trends of the time.

Miniskirts were worn with knee-high boots – called kinky or go-go boots – and tights rather than stockings.

Jean Shrimpton looking delicious

In 1965 the model Jean Shrimpton wore a miniskirt with no stockings, hat or gloves at the Melbourne Cup Carnival. It caused an instant stir among the middle-aged women wearing 'appropriate' clothing (yawn) that was a far cry from Jean's image of a young, carefree, super-cool gal.

In the late 60s the popularity of the miniskirt began to decline. Hemlines fell back to the ankle as fashion became more nostalgic, and feminists deemed the miniskirt the opposite of liberation. (Oh, bore off.)

But the end of the 70s saw the miniskirt re-emerge with the punk movement. Female rock stars like Debbie Harry were regularly seen in a mini. The counterculture fashions at this time railed against trends that were considered bourgeois, bland and over-indulgent. Around the same time, Vivienne Westwood and Malcolm McLaren reincarnated the miniskirt in leather and PVC with a trashy vibe.

During the 80s and 90s the miniskirt lived on. The power suit, which came with a miniskirt, was a wardrobe staple of the sophisticated, long-legged thirty-something career woman in control of her own life. The feminists had to have a rethink.

How to wear it

For a really cool way to wear a mini, keep the look relaxed and very hip so as not to look tarty. Miniskirts come in every fabric and print possible, so take your pick. Wear with a boyfriend shirt, or with a simple vest top underneath an oversized jumper or sweatshirt (I LOVE this look). For winter months, layer up with a Crombie or pea coat and accessorise with tights and ankle boots.

But please make sure you don't reveal too much cleavage if you are wearing a mini. The law with boobs and legs is that it's either/or.

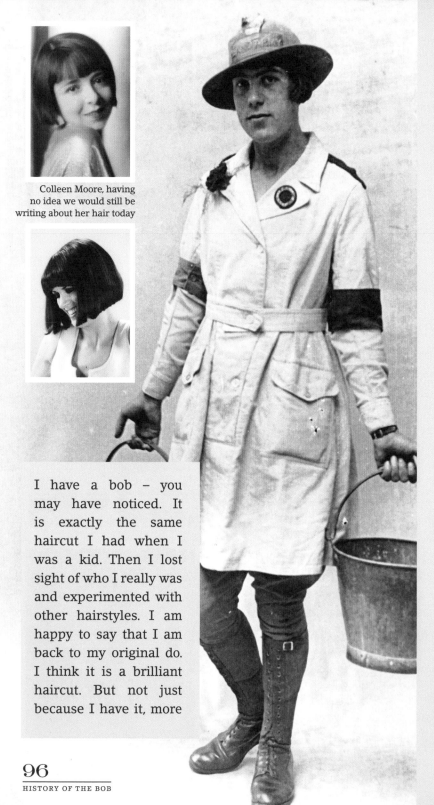

Colleen Moore, having no idea we would still be writing about her hair today

I have a bob – you may have noticed. It is exactly the same haircut I had when I was a kid. Then I lost sight of who I really was and experimented with other hairstyles. I am happy to say that I am back to my original do. I think it is a brilliant haircut. But not just because I have it, more

because of the journey it has been through over the last hundred years. So excuse me while I step away from clothes for a minute to talk about one of the most iconic hairstyles in history.

During the First World War women cut their hair shorter for practical reasons: they were taking on military duties. But that wasn't really a bob; it was just short hair. It was during the 20s that short hair became about fashion and the go-to do for any girl with a sense of style.

The Eton Crop, or Dutch Boy, was popularised by the It girl of the 20s, Louise Brooks – though it was first seen on long-forgotten actress Colleen Moore. The cut was short, close to the head and very dramatic. This was women abandoning the feminine stereotype and expressing their independence and daring intentions.

This was a very bold haircut and the start of Bob's journey, and he was

First World War landgirl

Vidal Sassoon giving Mary Quant a five-point cut

Anna Wintour, Editor of Vogue
and bob queen

to go through a lot to get to where he is today. (I just personified a haircut, I hope that isn't weird.)

Bob started to get more feminine over the 30s and 40s. His look was less severe, but although credited as having bobs, the likes of Bette Davis, Greta Garbo and Ginger Rogers really just had shorter hair. If you ask me, Bob went into hiding after the 20s but, man, did he ever make the comeback of all comebacks in the 60s.

In 1963 Vidal Sassoon gave Bob a second life in the five-point cut. He used the shape of the original bob and made it more stylish, simple and low-maintenance. It had five points to it. The purpose was that it would fall back perfectly into place, so aside from being super-stylish, it was also highly practical. It was a welcome relief from the curled and rollered dos of the decades before. Women had one less thing to think about with this cut, which is why it had such an impact in the 60s.

It was popularised by the likes of Mary Quant and Peggy Moffitt. And despite being a very retro design, it still feels very modern today.

In the 70s the pageboy cut was an alternative to long hippy locks. Worn by Joanna Lumley and Debbie Harry, it was Bob going through another identity crisis.

The 80s was probably Bob at his most confused. His back was shaved and sometimes the sides too, but from the front he was still himself. Popstars like Toyah Wilcox rocked this trend. The textured bob had a more layered, untidy look and the curly bob was big, as seen in Madonna's video for 'Express Yourself' in 1989.

But still, these personality traits were not Bob at his best. These days he exists in many forms, but the best can be seen on the likes of Anna Wintour, the editor of American *Vogue*. And of course Dora the Explorer, my personal style icon.

THE BRITISH CLOTHING MANUFACTURING INDUSTRY . . .
WHAT HAPPENED??

I love the labels in vintage clothes. So many of them say either 'Made in Britain', 'Made in London' or 'Made in the UK'. It's so rare to find the same accreditation in modern fashion, and I find that really sad. We have lost our manufacturing industry, but it used to be thriving. And although it would be impossible for larger brands to manufacture their clothes in the UK for the price of, say, in China, it's worth reminding ourselves to support those brands who do manage to keep it all on home soil. Maybe if we do that, one day it will come back. It needs to come back for so many reasons: unemployment here, horrible working conditions in foreign countries and our carbon footprint.

In the 20s, British textile production was in its prime, although cracks had started to develop during the First World War, when it became increasingly difficult to ship cotton to faraway places like Japan. So that meant over time those faraway places set up their own factories where manufacturing was much cheaper. Mills began to shut down in Britain, and the machinery was sent to countries like China and India to help them develop. So as Britain's textile production diminished, that of other countries started to thrive.

To this day the UK still can't compete with its overseas rivals. It's not just that we have none of the infrastructure left and it's more cost-effective to manufacture overseas, but also that the industry has been so quiet here for so long, it's now hard to find people with the right skills.

What a lot of higher-end brands do is the bulk of the manufacturing overseas, but then finish the clothes in the UK. This is, at least, a reasonable compromise. But it comes at a cost. And it is the consumer who ends up paying for it.

So the British fashion industry has been cornered. But of course manufacturing overseas comes with its own issues: awful working environments, excessive hours and workers often denied basic union rights.

So what to do?

Just support brands that are made in Britain as much as you can. Hopefully, if we do that, then things will start to change. And, of course, shop vintage and enjoy the millions of amazing items that already exist, to take the load off those workers out in China, India and everywhere else who work epic shifts in shocking conditions so that we can look pretty.

DESIGNER VINTAGE

One truly thrilling part of vintage shopping is finding a piece of designer clothing that is not only an important part of fashion history, but also worth a few quid. I am always on the lookout for designer pieces, my personal favourites being Ossie Clark, Mary Quant, André Courrèges, Pierre Cardin, Susan Small, Chanel, Pucci . . . Oh my, there are just too many to mention.

Each designer from the past set the imprint for the fashion of the future. Their work is as beautiful as it is fascinating, and I couldn't write this book without explaining to you why, and how you can find your own.

No one is as qualified in the world of designer vintage as William Banks-Blaney. Named by *Vogue* as The Vintage King, William runs a store called WilliamVintage. He sells some of the most exquisite designer vintage clothing and haute couture in the world. In fairness, he taught me most of what I know, so what better than to have the man himself talk about designer vintage?

The key to buying designer vintage is knowing which designers to look for. Who are your favourites?

I have so many, but I think there are some designers who brought something new to clothing and who really had something to say about women and how they could dress. Dior for his New Look with his nipped waists and full skirts, Yves Saint Laurent for the way he changed the accessibility of fashion with prêt-à-porter and Chanel for her suits and for challenging notions of what women's clothing could be. That said, my obsession above all else is Balenciaga.

Why's that?

Cristóbal Balenciaga was extraordinary. He is the man Coco Chanel called 'The Master' and whom nearly every other designer refers to as 'the couturier's couturier'. His understanding of fabric, and the way he incorporated inspirations and influences within his clothing, as well as his general approach to clothes and to women, really makes him stand out. His designs are spectacular, and clearly show that he loved women as much for their strength as their beauty, and they remain amazingly contemporary.

Where do you find most of your designer vintage?

I travel constantly to find the best; the key to WilliamVintage is the edit of pieces that are not only in great condition, but also still have relevance for a woman today – and that's a tough brief to fulfil. Dresses tend to travel, as they get forgotten in attics or are given away to friends (or, in the grander houses, to domestic staff), so I never rule out any locales. I buy from private families, from dealers around the world who scout for me, from museums who are discreetly selling parts of their collections . . . Everyone has clothes, so therefore anyone may have something I want.

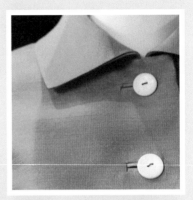

Can anyone just rock up to an auction? I'd be scared I might accidentally blow three million on a blouse from Topshop.

The vast majority of auctions are open to the public, and while there are several geared solely towards vintage clothing, you will often find random vintage clothing in many regional auction houses. They can be interesting and can also lead to some really terrific finds. My words of warning when buying from an auction are to always inspect the pieces before you bid, rather than relying on a picture, and to not get carried away in the frenzy of bidding, which is incredibly easy to do.

So what are you looking for when you go hunting?

Put simply, I look for clothing that I like. I specialise in vintage haute couture, but I am not a label snob, so if I find something amazing that I think is still relevant, different

and with a story left to tell, I buy it. Condition, condition, condition is key for me.

You know how in *Point Break* there was the ultimate wave, is there the ultimate dress?

My ultimate? Despite not selling any bridal dresses, my ultimate is the 1967 Balenciaga wedding dress in white silk gazar . . . It's my Holy Grail and perfection in a dress. Or the 1920 'Light' dress made for Luisa Casati by Charles Frederick Worth, made of chiffon and real diamonds. That has been lost for over sixty years. I want that dress!

I am lucky to have had a lot of ultimates already: the original 1926 Chanel LBD, the 1954 Dior 'Elisabeth' ball gown, the 1968 Courrèges dress used in the *Vogue* shoot that went on to be one of the greatest fashion images of all time. I've been lucky!

What are the things to be wary of when shopping for designer vintage?

Firstly, don't buy something that has a missing button, missing beading or very old staining and assume you can fix it. Secondly, if you are spending a decent amount of money on a piece, make sure it is from a dealer with a good reputation, and be wary of anything that relies on a dealer promising you it's a particular thing. Unless you are a real expert or a specialist, if someone is trying to sell you an 'unlabelled Dior', I would suggest you err on the side of caution.

What should people be looking for inside the clothes? What details? What are the signs that it is couture?

The first thing I do when considering buying a dress is to turn it inside out. Any hidden repairs, holes, patches or alterations are immediately apparent, so the inside of a dress is hugely important, particularly if it is a more expensive piece. A couture piece will have a superb inside finish level, so look for generous selvedges [seams], interior waistbands, in-built corsets and hand-stitching of a very fine level.

All designers have a language and I always advise women to ease their way into vintage and to try and learn as they go…The sharp silhouette of a Courrèges, the crispness of an Yves Saint Laurent shoulder, the knife-pleating of a Dior … There are usually lots of signatures on a dress by a great designer, so if you have seen something you love and want to learn more, read about it, look at images of other pieces by that designer or get a second opinion.

How do you know it's worth something? Surely a lot of scamming goes on?

There are obvious signs for something of value; anything with an important label, of course. However, be careful, as these dresses can be forty, fifty, sixty or more years old and labels can get lost, so just because it doesn't have one may not mean it's worthless. If you think you may have found something really special, ask an expert.

Does an item lose value if it has been altered?

Without question, yes, though the degree to which it loses value depends on the dress and what has been done to it. For example, a generic 60s dress will not be wildly affected if you tailor it a little. My rule of thumb is: don't buy a maxi to make into a mini, in the same way that you wouldn't chop the legs off a Chippendale desk to make it into a coffee table. I have seen some alteration disasters, such as a wonderful 50s couture dress that was deemed out of date in the 70s so was chopped and changed and which now, if it had been left alone, would be priceless.

What would stop you buying something?

If I love a dress, I will move heaven and earth to make it mine, and the only real issue would be condition. I have bought exceptional pieces that needed some TLC, but there has to be a line and I only cross it if I feel the dress may be lost unless I intercede. For example, I once found a beautiful 50s Dior haute couture dress that was in a perilous state: the ivory silk was black with dirt and smoke damage, the silk threads securing the amazing beading were rotting . . . the dress was on its last legs. But I have access to museum-grade cleaners and trained couture seamstresses, and I loved it, so I decided to save it. An indication of the love I had for it is that just cleaning the dress took six weeks and cost £1,800.

Why is a garment worth so much even though it's old?

Why is antique furniture worth more than modern furniture? Why is a vintage Rolls-Royce cooler than a modern one? It's because at the higher end of any market are rare, beautifully made things designed by someone who achieved world-acclaim for what they did. It's easy to forget that the super-brands of Chanel, Dior, Saint Laurent, Balmain and Givenchy all started with one man or woman with a vision, and vintage pieces by the great designers are the bible, the proof, the evidence of what made them great.

Also, it's not just something to hang on your wall, but rather something you can wear, therefore a much more immediate, intimate way of enjoying something really beautiful. That's the sexiest form of art, no?

How should people look after their designer vintage?

Find a good dry-cleaner, invest in good hangers and think about the piece itself. A Rahvis silk chiffon dress is too delicate to wear three times a week, but an Ossie Clark moss crêpe one is resilient enough to wear almost constantly, so don't ask a dress to do more than it can. I have seen so many dresses with sleeves ripped by wire hangers or fine fabrics that have worn through or faded due to overwear.

Where is the strangest place you have ever found a gem?

I once opened the doors of a cheap vinyl wardrobe in a barn in Devon to find fourteen pieces of the 1967 Courrèges haute couture collection, in perfect condition and only worn once. That was an epic day.

What is your favourite discovery of your career?

Oh, I have so many! One was not the most valuable piece but it was perhaps the most romantic. It was a very beautiful, very sexy 60s Chanel LBD and it had a tricky rear zipper. As I was zipping a client into the dress, we were discussing that the last time the dress had been worn, the original owner's husband had

probably had to do the same thing. She bought the dress the second I mentioned that it had belonged to Mrs Nat King Cole, and that the last man to have his hands on the zipper was probably 'Velvet Voice' himself. A little moment of magic right there.

How much of what you buy gets bought by museums?

I have very strong relationships with most of the world's major museums. They are incredibly exacting and only interested in the very finest pieces, which are iconic of the designer, in exceptional unaltered condition.

How do you know when a piece should go into a museum? I mean, would some items be wasted in someone's wardrobe?

My buzz will always come from seeing a woman wearing a dress, no matter how important or valuable the dress may be, because that is what it was made for. However, my clients range from private buyers who want to wear the dresses to museums and archives and fashion designers, so I know that my discoveries will always end up in an environment where they are appreciated one way or another, and that keeps me happy.

I don't think it's about a dress in a wardrobe being 'wasted', but it can be lovely when I find something really exceptional to know that it will make someone gasp with delight every single day, once it is beautifully lit and on display somewhere.

How much do you sell to today's designers looking for shapes and inspiration? Do many designers use clothes from the vintage decades to inspire their new collections?

A revelation for so many of my clients is that when they start to look at vintage clothing, they already recognise the shapes from contemporary collections. Designers have always looked to the past for silhouettes, details and moods, and I find they buy a great deal of vintage

for their own inspiration. Fashion might not be about reinventing the wheel, but it is about shaping what we wear through our memories, through romantic ideas and through moods that are easily found and translated from vintage clothing.

Why is haute couture so expensive, when you could pop to the local dry-cleaners and get something made to fit you perfectly?

There is a great difference between having something tailored to fit you and having something created for you from scratch. An haute couture dress will first be made for you in cotton and will go through several fittings to ensure the size and shape of the panels is perfect on your body [this cotton version is known as the toile]. Once the dress has been accurately 'sketched', the same process then begins with the final fabric. A dress may involve a team of pattern-cutters, a team of seamstresses, then a separate team of chiffon workers and then a team of embroiderers, so the level of work that goes into one unique dress can be several thousand hours for a complex piece. In addition to the expert labour involved in the dress, its starting point is also the idea of a creative genius.

Any final nuggets of advice?

Don't forget to enjoy shopping! If the process, store, dress or sales assistant makes you feel anything other than happy, walk away, because someone isn't doing their job properly.

SOME DESIGNERS TO LOOK OUT FOR . . .

20S

Jean Patou

A French designer specialising in sportswear. He was the first designer to put his monogram on his clothes: a J and a P outlining the pockets.

Elsa Schiaparelli

An Italian designer, seen as Coco Chanel's biggest rival. She became famous for her cravat knit sweaters.

Coco Chanel

Responsible for the women's suit and the Little Black Dress, a simple classic still seen today.

30S

Robert Piguet

A French designer who embraced theatrical 30s romanticism, incorporating high cap sleeves, large yokes and high collars.

Madame Grès

A French designer known for her draping techniques.

Mainbocher

American designer who created Wallis Simpson's two-piece crêpe wedding dress, and popularised the colour 'Wallis blue'.

Madeleine Vionnet

Like Madame Grès, she favoured draping and bias-cuts, and she made the halter silhouette and cowl neck popular.

40S

Christian Dior

His New Look revolutionised late-40s fashion.

Norman Hartnell

A British dress designer and royal warrant dressmaker to the Queen and Queen Mother.

Nina Ricci

A French designer known for her refined and feminine designs.

50S

Pierre Balmain

A French designer known for elegance and grace, and for popularising the stole.

Jacques Fath

The 'little prince of haute couture'.

Cristóbal Balenciaga

A Spanish designer who changed the 50s silhouette by removing the waist and broadening the shoulders.

60S

Mary Quant

British fashion designer and icon who brought in the miniskirt and hot pants, and became instrumental in mod fashion.

Biba

A fashion label run in London by Polish-born Barbara Hulanicki. Her designs inspired the transition from the 60s to the 70s.

Pierre Cardin

A French designer known for his avant-garde style and his logo displayed on his clothes.

Yves Saint Laurent

Popularised many fashion trends, such as safari jackets and the Mondrian shift dress.

Pucci

An Italian designer known for geometric, psychedelic prints.

70S

Vivienne Westwood

A British designer whose clothes shaped the British punk scene.

Laura Ashley

A British designer known for high-necked blouses and long, flounced skirts, as well as floral prints.

Diane von Furstenberg

Belgian-born American designer. She became famous for the design of the wrap dress.

Roy Halston Frowick

American designer, famous for trouser suits and jersey dresses, as well as turtle-neck jumpers.

80S

Giorgio Armani

Known for branching out into other products, such as socks and sunglasses, the Italian designer was one of the big brands of the 80s.

Ralph Lauren

Responsible for the American preppy look that is still strong today.

Calvin Klein

Arguably revolutionised how people saw their underwear – and jeans. Also famous for clean, sophisticated 'New York' fashion.

Jean Paul Gaultier

A French designer known for his somewhat crazy style. He designed Madonna's outfits for her Blond Ambition tour, including the infamous cone bra.

Betty Jackson

Her Victorian influences helped integrate vintage style into more popular trends.

And Bill Gibb, Jean Varon, Leonard, Sybil Connolly, Givenchy, Gucci, Paco Rabanne, Prada, Susan Small, Claire McCardell . . . Oh, there are so many more and I have run out of space . . .

WHEN TO TAKE IT TO A TAILOR
AND WHEN TO TRY IT YOURSELF

I can't sew to save my life. The last thing I made was a rent-a-tent nightie at school. The main thing I remember about it was forgetting to take it into class one day, and being really scared of my teacher because she was so strict. So I told her I was sick on it the night before. She then told me to go home and eat dry toast. And that was about it for my sewing education.

I am now taking occasional lessons, just to learn the little bits that I often ask tailors to do that I really should be doing myself. It's fun, and I have no intention of being sick on any of the things I have fixed. Which is a good sign.

I highly recommend sewing lessons if you buy a lot of vintage, because very often items need a little bit of work. However, I will say that, for the bigger jobs, it is important you find a tailor you trust. These clothes are old and one of a kind, so don't risk ruining them just to save a couple of quid if you don't know how to do it.

My tailor in London is the guy in my local dry cleaner. He isn't expensive and he does a great job.

One thing you must always remember, though, is never let them cut away the material if they are taking in a dress, top or waistband. Or anything, for that matter.

The best thing about vintage pieces is the seam allowances. Dresses were designed to go in and out with the woman, so if you buy something that is too big and you want the tailor to take it in, you need them to keep that fabric inside in case you ever need it taken out again. This way, dresses last you forever. These seam allowances are not something you see very often on the high street; they are a very important reason why vintage is best, so hold onto the fabric. You will be grateful after Christmas when you need a few more inches let out so you can breathe.

Also, always make sure you have proper fittings, and don't rush the process. You are paying for the service, so make sure they pin it properly and that you are happy before they start unpicking.

DIY WARDROBE WORKSHOP

If you do fancy getting crafty, here are some brilliant ways to revamp your clothes. Just go easy with the scissors and don't blame me if it all goes wrong.

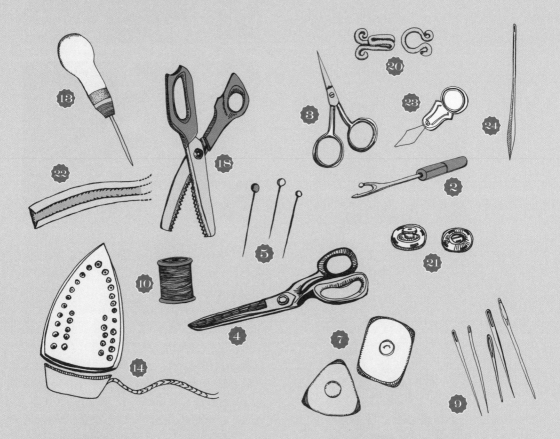

GET EQUIPPED

1. Sewing machine with different stitch settings
2. Stitch unpicker
3. Fine scissors
4. Fabric scissors
5. Pins
6. Safety pins
7. Tailor's chalk
8. Tape measure
9. Needles in a selection of sizes
10. Sewing thread in various colours
11. Pencil
12. Scrap paper

ALSO USEFUL

13. Awl
14. Iron (with steaming function)
15. Ironing board
16. Scrap fabric
17. Hairdryer
18. Pinking shears
19. Fusible web
20. Hooks and eyes
21. Press studs
22. Bias binding
23. Needle threader
24. Leather needle

① THREAD A NEEDLE

YOU WILL NEED

• a needle • thread • fine scissors • needle threader (optional)

HOW TO START

1. Choose a needle with the right size hole for your thread

2. Cut a suitable length of thread: too short and it will run out too soon; too long and it might get tangled in your work

HOW TO THREAD BY HAND

1. Hold the needle between your thumb and forefinger with the eye pointing upwards

2. Hold the thread between your other thumb and forefinger, 1cm from the end

3. Insert the tip of the thread through the eye

4. Pull through several centimetres of thread so a generous tail hangs down

HOW TO USE A NEEDLE THREADER

1. Hold the needle in one hand and the needle threader in the other

2. Insert the pointed end of the threader through the eye of the needle

3. Insert the thread through the thin loop of the threader

4. Pull the threader loop (and thread) back through the eye of the needle

HINT
Keep an eye out to make sure you are only sewing with single thread and not including the tail

HINT
Cut the thread at 45 degrees to give a sharper point for threading

HINT
Ensure your work area is well lit

HINT
Wet the tip of the thread with your tongue to make it stiffer and easier to thread

② SEW ON A BUTTON

YOU WILL NEED

• thread in a matching or complementary colour • a sharp needle • buttons • a pin

HOW TO

1. Thread the needle

2. Position the button on the garment, testing it fits inside its buttonhole

3. Insert the needle through the garment from the inside and pull it all the way through, leaving a small tail on the reverse

4. Secure the thread by making 2 or 3 small stitches in the same spot over the tail-end of the thread

5. For a sew-through button, push the needle and thread up through one hole of the button

6. Insert a pin beneath the button, between the stitch you've made and where the next stitch will go. (This will stop the button from being sewn on too tightly.)

7. Thread the needle down into the next hole of the button, through the material and then up through a different hole. If using a two-hole button, you always go up through the same hole and down through the other. If using a four-hole button, you can choose the pattern you create.

8. For a shank button, push the needle from the wrong side of the fabric, through the shank, pulling the thread all the way

9. With the thread through the shank, create a stitch where the button should be fixed and tighten it

10. Repeat the process until the button is secure

11. On the last stitch, push the needle through the fabric but not the button/shank

12. For sew-through buttons, remove the pin

13. Wrap the thread between the button and material six times to reinforce the shank

14. Push the needle back down through the material

15. On the reverse of the fabric make 3 or 4 small stitches to secure the thread

16. Tie the thread and cut off excess

HINT

Use double thread to make the job quicker and the button more secure

③ TAPER TROUSERS / JEANS

HINT

If you don't have pinking shears, cut with scissors and zigzag sew to prevent fraying

YOU WILL NEED

• a helper • pins • stitch unpicker • tailor's chalk • sewing machine • thread in contrasting/matching colour as desired • pinking shears • iron

HOW TO

1. Put the trousers on inside out and decide where the tapering should start

2. Have your helper pin the new shape by taking in the excess fabric at the seams

3. Remove trousers (carefully – don't get pin-pricked)

4. Use the stitch unpicker to take down the hem

5. Mark the tapering lines in tailor's chalk

6. Press with iron

7. Machine sew along chalk lines

8. Cut excess fabric away with pinking shears, leaving 1cm seam allowance

9. Iron seams flat

10. Machine sew bottom hems in place as before

④ TURN A TOP INTO A JACKET / WAISTCOAT

HINT

See 'Stop fraying' to check your material won't fray

YOU WILL NEED

• tape measure • tailor's chalk • bias binding at least twice the length of the garment • sewing machine • thread in matching colour • scissors • needle

HOW TO

1. Use the tape measure to find the midpoint of the neck and midpoint of the bottom edge of the garment

2. Using tailor's chalk, mark a line vertically down the centre of the garment

3. Pin bias binding on one side of the centre mark, with the edge 5mm away from the chalk mark, right sides together

4. Machine sew along the fold in the bias binding

5. Repeat on the other side

6. Cut down chalk line between the two biases

7. On each side, fold binding to the inside and pin in place (ensure the edge is tucked inside at the fold)

8. Hand-sew binding in place on the reverse to finish

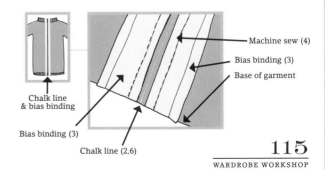

Chalk line & bias binding

Bias binding (3)

Chalk line (2,6)

Machine sew (4)

Bias binding (3)

Base of garment

STOP FRAYING

Seams on factory-made clothes are usually finished with a machine called an overlocker to stop them fraying. Standard sewing machines don't often have overlocking devices, but you can do the same with the zigzag setting on your sewing machine.

YOU WILL NEED

• sewing machine • thread in matching colour

HOW TO

1. Set your sewing machine to the smallest-size zigzag stitch

2. Before you start sewing seams, machine-sew right along the edge of the fabric

3. Sew seams as usual

HINT

Cut ribbons diagonally to stop them fraying

HINT

Some fabrics don't fray! So don't worry about polyjersey, felt or fleece, or the selvedges (finished edges) of fabrics

HINT

Cut fabric with pinking shears if you have no sewing machine

Overlocked edge   Zigzagged edge

TAKE DOWN A HEM

YOU WILL NEED

• fine scissors • stitch unpicker • iron

HOW TO

1. Turn the garment inside out

2. Carefully snip one stitch holding up the hem

3. Use the stitch unpicker to remove the hem stitches

4. You may need to start with a new snip at a few places as you go

5. Remove all loose threads

6. Pull the hem down and use the iron to remove the crease

7. See 'Shorten a dress/skirt' for how to add in a new hem if desired

HINT

Vintage garments can be faded, meaning that the hem fabric could be brighter than the main fabric

7 COVER BUTTONS WITH FABRIC

YOU WILL NEED

• scissors • fabric • needle • sewing thread in any colour • domed coverable buttons in the right size for the buttonholes

HOW TO

1. Cut a square of fabric about 1cm bigger than the buttonall round

2. Trim off the corners to give a rough circle shape, still bigger than the button

3. Thread the needle and sew a tacking stitch around the edge of the fabric with two long ends left

4. Place the 'dome' of the button into the wrong side of the fabric

5. Pull the two thread ends to tighten the fabric around the button (like a shower cap)

6. When covered, snap on the button's back fastening

TACKING STITCH

1. Tie a knot at the end of the thread

2. Make a series of long running stitches. Choose a stitch length that is short enough to secure the fabric for as long as you need it to, but long enough to be easy to remove when no longer needed

3. Fasten the end loosely with a knot

WRONG OR RIGHT?

The 'right' side of a fabric has the clearest side of the print/design on show. The 'wrong' side looks . . . wrong. Sometimes it is hard to tell which is which; look carefully for clues.

8 REPAIR MOTH HOLES

YOU WILL NEED

• stitch unpicker • scissors • fusible web • iron/steamer

HOW TO

1. If the garment is lined, unpick the lining enough to allow you to gain access to the reverse of the moth holes

2. Check around the inside of the garment for any excess material (hem and cuff areas are likely places)

3. Cut out a patch of excess fabric around 2cm wider than the moth hole

4. From the wrong side of the fabric, carefully place fusible web around the outside of the hole (not over it)

5. Steam the fusible web on to secure

6. Place the patch fabric over the hole and iron for 30 seconds to fuse it in place

⑨ DIP-DYE FABRIC

YOU WILL NEED

• rubber gloves • 8 tablespoons of salt (table salt is fine) • jug • 6 litres of hot water • fabric dye in chosen colour • washing-up bowl • spoon • hairdryer

HOW TO

1. Dissolve the salt into 500ml hot water

2. Add dye to the hot salty water and stir well to dissolve

3. Pour the jug of dissolved dye/salt into the rest of the hot water in the washing-up bowl and stir well

4. Dampen your garment in normal water

5. Immerse the bottom section of your garment in the dye and hold it there for about 5 minutes

6. Lower in the next section of the garment and hold for about 3 minutes

7. Add in the next section for a further 1 minute

8. Submerge the whole garment for 30 seconds, stirring it around in the dye

9. Check the colour, then wring out the garment and rinse under cold running water

10. Hang or lie the garment flat to dry until just damp

11. For a mottled effect, sprinkle leftover dye powder over the damp garment and dry it on with a hairdryer; don't wash it off

12. For the first couple of washes, hand-wash cold or use a fixing solution – the colour will run at first

NOTE

1. If your garment isn't white to start with, bleach the fabric first. You can add 175ml bleach to the laundry liquid dispenser of your machine and use the hottest wash you can.

2. Fabrics won't take dye if they are more than 50% polyester, made from acrylic, acetate or water-repellent fabrics, or marked 'dry clean only'

HINT
There are separate fabric dyes for hand-dyeing and machine-dyeing; make sure you choose the right one for your project

HINT
By hand-dyeing you can create effects – and there are often better colours available

HINT
Machine-dyeing is easier and the best way to dye large items like jeans to get an even overall colour

10 CUSTOMISE WITH PRINTS

HINT
Test whether your fabric can stand being ironed by ironing on an inconspicuous test patch first

YOU WILL NEED

• scissors • fabric print of your choice • iron • paper-backed fusible web
• sewing machine • thread in contrasting colour

HOW TO

1. Cut out the fabric image you want to transfer, leaving a large border

2. Iron the fusible web onto the back of the fabric image

3. Cut away the border around the image

4. Peel off the paper backing

5. Put the garment flat on an ironing board

6. Position the fabric image glue-side down where wanted

7. Iron the patch to bond it in place

8. If the garment is lined, unpick the lining and access the reverse of the garment where the fabric has been applied

9. Using a wide zigzag stitch, machine sew around the cut edge of the patch on the right side, taking care to avoid sewing over the lining

10. Replace and sew up the lining

11 TURN A FLOATY SKIRT INTO A WIGGLE SKIRT

YOU WILL NEED

• a helper • safety pins/dressmaker's pins • tailor's chalk • stitch unpicker
• sewing machine • thread in matching colour • scissors

HOW TO

1. Turn the garment inside out and put it on

2. With your helper assisting, reshape the skirt by using safety pins to pin away the excess along the side seams. The bottom of the skirt should be narrower than the waist.

3. Adjust until you are happy with the fit

4. Take off the dress/skirt

5. Mark the pin positions in tailor's chalk

6. Remove the pins

7. Unpick the hem turnings where the new seams are to go (leave the hems untouched at the areas that won't be adapted)

8. Machine-sew along marked lines

9. Try the garment on and adjust if necessary

10. Cut away excess fabric from the new seams, leaving 1cm seam allowance

11. Machine-sew with zigzag stitch along the raw edges to stop fraying

12. Hand-sew the hem turning back in place

⑫ LET OUT FABRIC FOR A BIGGER SIZE

Vintage garments often have extra seam allowance on the inside, which you can use to expand if it is a bit tight.

YOU WILL NEED

• a helper • pins • tape measure • stitch unpicker • sewing machine
• thread in matching colour

HOW TO

1. Put the garment on

2. Ask your helper to pin where it feels tight by placing two pins horizontally to the seam to mark where you will need to let it out. Try to pin equally on each side.

3. Take the garment off and if the garment is lined, unpick the hem to release the lining and reveal the seams

4. Starting at the waist, unpick the seam between the horizontal pins

5. Repeat for all marked seams

6. Sew new seams, tapering from the original start point out to the new position, and back in to meet at the original end point

7. Turn the garment the right way round and press with an iron

8. Turn the skirt hem back to its original length and sew to secure (see 'Shorten a dress/skirt')

9. Turn the lining hem, if there, back to original length and sew to secure

10. Press to finish

HINT
Check the fabric won't be marked where you let out the stitches

HINT
It is usually better to take more fabric out of side seams than front seams

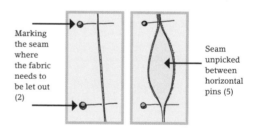

Marking the seam where the fabric needs to be let out (2)

Seam unpicked between horizontal pins (5)

⑬ REMOVE SHOULDER PADS

YOU WILL NEED

• stitch unpicker
• thread in matching colour
• a needle

HOW TO

1. If the garment is lined, unpick the lining stitching to gain access to the pads

2. Unpick stitches attaching the pad to the garment, and remove the pad and any loose threads

3. Hand-stitch the lining back in place

STOP ZIPS COMING UNDONE

YOU WILL NEED

• a sharp needle • sewing thread in matching colour • hook and eye

HOW TO

1. Thread the needle with thread to match garment

2. Sew the 'hook' at the top of one side of the zip. Fasten with a few stitches in the same spot.

3. Sew the 'eye' at the top of the other side of the zip, fastening in the same way

 ## CUT OFF DENIM SHORTS

YOU WILL NEED

• a helper • pins • tape measure • tailor's chalk • scissors

HOW TO

1. Wearing the jeans, and with your helper, mark the length you want the shorts with a pin at the crotch and another at the side seam

2. Take off the jeans and measure the length from the waistband down to the pins on one leg

3. Copy the measurements onto the other leg

4. Draw a chalk line matching up the measurements

5. Cut along the chalk line if you are going to zigzag sew the raw edge, or 1cm lower than the chalk line if you are going to leave it to fray

HINT
It's much easier to mark your jeans accurately with a helper

HINT
You can speed up the fraying by pulling a few strands loose from the cut edge

HINT
The cut-off look is more flattering if the side length is slightly shorter than at the crotch

HINT
Make your first cut longer than you want, and work up

16 SHORTEN A DRESS / SKIRT

YOU WILL NEED

• pins • tailor's chalk • scissors • iron • sewing machine • thread in matching colour

HOW TO

1. Put on the dress/skirt

2. Choose your desired length and insert pins in a horizontal line to mark. This is easier with someone to help, but on your own check the level of the pin lines in the mirror and adjust if needed.

3. Remove the dress/skirt

4. Lie it on a flat surface to check dress (and lining, if present) is flat and straight

5. Choose your hem length

6. Use the tailor's chalk to mark the line of your chosen hem allowance below the pinned line

7. Carefully cut along the chalk line and remove excess fabric

8. Fold up 2cm for a single-folded hem, or 1cm for the first part of a double-folded hem, and press with an iron

9. Machine-sew 2mm below the top of the turned-up edge

10. Fold and press another 1cm turn (if using)

11. Machine- or hand-sew the hem turning in place

12. If the dress/skirt is lined, repeat steps for the lining, to end up 25mm shorter than the skirt hem

HINT
To ensure you are pinning a straight new hemline, when wearing the garment, measure from the floor up

HINT
To ensure the hem is invisible from the front, hand-sew it with a slip stitch, or use a hemming foot on your sewing machine

HINT
If you are using a single-folded hem, see 'Stop fraying' to ensure the fabric won't fray

HINT
Keep hold of the cut-away fabric. You never know when you might need it to patch a hole – or if you have enough, you could use it to make a belt, bow or to cover buttons

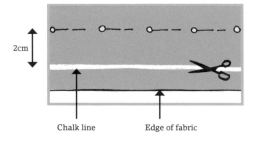

2cm

Chalk line   Edge of fabric

17 DECIDE WHAT LENGTH HEM TO USE

Hem length will typically be between 1.5cm and 7.5cm.

TYPES OF HEM

1. Single turn: where the hem is folded up once, so the raw edge is visible on the reverse of the garment. Suitable for creating a light hem on delicate fabrics and lower-quality garments.

2. Double turn: where the bottom edge is folded up twice so the raw edge is tucked into the hem and not visible. Makes the hem neater and creates a 'heavier' bottom edge.

3. Rolled hem: where the bottom edge is folded up 5mm and sewn over with larger stitches, which are then pulled to make the fabric roll over into a tiny hem. Used on very fine fabrics such as silk or chiffon.

THE LENGTH YOU CHOOSE IS UP TO YOU, DEPENDING ON

1. The amount of excess fabric available

2. The weight of the fabric: the more fabric you turn up, the heavier the 'pull' down on the garment, which can be useful for pulling the garment into shape. Or, if you wish to allow light fabric to be floaty, you'll want a light hem using as little fabric as possible.

3. The quality of the garment: good-quality garments deserve good-quality hems and should be double-turned

18 REMOVE STAINS

YOU WILL NEED

• fabric stain remover spray • cotton cloth • hairdryer

HOW TO

1. Spray on the stain remover and rub in gently with the cotton cloth

2. Leave to soak in for 5 minutes

3. Rinse the stained area under cold running water for 2 minutes

4. Wring out the fabric, then rinse again

5. Hang up the garment and blast it with a hot hairdryer for 5 minutes

6. Leave garment to cool for 5 minutes

7. Repeat with heating/cooling steps until the garment is dry to touch

8. Iron the garment to remove any creases

LOWER A NECKLINE

YOU WILL NEED

• tailor's chalk • tape measure • scissors
• bias binding to complement fabric
• pins • sewing machine • thread in
matching colour

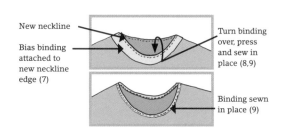

New neckline

Bias binding attached to new neckline edge (7)

Turn binding over, press and sew in place (8,9)

Binding sewn in place (9)

HOW TO

1. Draw rough desired neckline onto the fabric in tailor's chalk

2. When happy, take measurements from one side only in key places

3. Transfer measurements to the other side to ensure the shape is even

4. Mark a seam allowance of a further 1cm bigger than you want the final neckline to be

5. Cut out the new neck shape along the marked outer allowance

6. Open bias binding and pin one edge, right sides together, along the raw neckline edge

7. Machine-sew binding in place

8. Turn binding over onto the inside of the neckline and press flat, far enough down that you can't see the binding from the front of the garment

9. Machine-sew binding in place by sewing along right side of the fabric

APPLY CRYSTALS / JEWELS / BEADS

YOU WILL NEED

• sew-on crystals/jewels/beads • tailor's chalk (ideally in pencil format) • a sharp needle • very strong thread

HOW TO

1. Lie the clothing to be decorated flat on a smooth surface

2. Spread the crystals/jewels/beads around until you are happy with their placement, be it random or structured

3. Take a photo of the pattern for reference

4. Use tailor's chalk to mark position of each crystal/jewel/bead on garment

5. Remove embellishments from the garment (keep them safe!)

6. Sew each crystal/jewel/bead firmly in place using very strong thread

HINT
If your garment has a lining, pin it in place to stop it moving about when you sew on the embellishments

HINT
Sew each crystal/jewel/bead on separately so that if you lose one, the others remain secure

21 REMOVE CRYSTALS / JEWELS / BEADS

Glass beads are likely to break a sewing-machine needle, so if you are planning on machine-sewing a beaded garment, make sure you remove any glass beads from the area to be stitched. (Plastic sequins, however, are fine to sew over.)

If there are lots of beads to remove that have been sewn on with one continuous stitch, it is easier to smash the individual beads rather than unravel a large amount of sewing.

YOU WILL NEED

• old bread board/chopping board • scrap fabric (ideally transparent) or a plastic bag • small hammer (such as a toffee hammer)

HOW TO

1. Put the garment on a chopping board or other hard, clean surface that's not too precious

2. Place scrap fabric over the beads

3. Use the hammer to smash all unwanted beads

4. Clear away the broken beads and discard

5. Vacuum-clean around the area to pick up any overlooked pieces

NOTE

Smashing beads can be dangerous! Ensure all beads are covered before you smash them and wear protective eyewear.

22 APPLY RHINESTONES

HINT

Take care because the end of the wand gets very hot!

YOU WILL NEED

• hot-fix rhinestones in chosen colours/sizes • tailor's chalk (pencil format) • hot-fix wand

HOW TO

1. Decide where you want to position your rhinestones – in a random or formal pattern

2. When happy, take a photo for reference

3. Mark position of each rhinestone on the garment with tailor's chalk, removing each one as you go

4. Make sure you have the correct size head on the wand to match the rhinestone size

5. Turn on the wand to heat up

6. Place a crystal on the fabric, hold the hot wand over the crystal and press down, holding still for 5 seconds

7. Repeat until all the rhinestones have been applied, changing the size of the wand head if you change rhinestone size

23 MAKE A BELT OUT OF EXCESS FABRIC

YOU WILL NEED

• excess fabric off-cut • scissors • sewing machine • complementary thread • iron • awl (or a chopstick or knitting needle)

HOW TO

To find the desired length:

1. Measure your waist with a tape measure

2. Add an extra 90cm for tying the belt in a bow

To extend the length of your fabric:

1. Cut fabric in half lengthways

2. Place 2 lengths of fabric together, right sides facing, and sew short ends together 5mm from the edge

3. Press the seam open

4. Fold the belt in half along the short edge, right sides together, to find the midpoint

5. Place 2 pins horizontally 5cm from the midpoint on each side

6. Fold the belt in half along the long side, right sides together, to make a long strip

7. Pin edges together and sew along 3 sides, leaving a 5mm seam all around, but leaving a gap between the 2 pins

8. Snip away excess fabric diagonally at each corner (but don't go too close to the stitches)

9. Turn the belt inside out through the gap, using a pointy instrument like a knitting needle to poke out all the corners

10. Hand-stitch the hole closed

11. Press with an iron

NOTE

The amount of fabric you have will determine how wide/long the belt is

HINT

Sewing 2 short ends together is better done at an angle rather than at right-angles to the edge

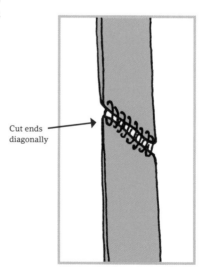

Cut ends diagonally

TAKE IN A LARGE JACKET

YOU WILL NEED

• a helper • pins • stitch unpicker • tailor's chalk • sewing machine • complementary thread • scissors • iron

HOW TO

1. Put the jacket on inside out

2. With your helper, put pins in the side seams to bring the jacket into a more fitting shape

3. Take off the jacket (carefully)

4. Use the stitch unpicker to unpick jacket lining (if present) to get access to inner side seams

5. Repin the jacket on the inside (without the lining) and use tailor's chalk to mark the new seam lines

6. Remove the pins

7. Machine-sew along new seam lines

8. Use scissors to nip cuts into the excess fabric (don't go too close to the stitches)

9. Repeat steps 1 – 8 to taper the sleeves

10. Sew the lining back in place

11. Press with a hot iron to finish

NOTE

1. Snipping into the fabric excess at the seam allows the fabric to sit smoothly and not pull the garment out of line

2. Taking the time to sew the lining in place by hand will mean it's invisible from the right side

 ## HOW TO USE A STITCH UNPICKER

YOU WILL NEED

• stitch unpicker • fine scissors

HOW TO

1. Insert the long end of the stitch unpicker under one of the stitches

2. Carefully push the unpicker along the row of stitches, allowing the sharp curved edge to cut the threads

3. <u>Take care</u> to make sure you aren't damaging any of the fabric as you go

4. Use scissors to snip any snagging thread

5. Pick out the loose ends of cut thread

MAKE A PETER PAN COLLAR

This is a good way to update an overly large existing collar, or to add a new point of interest to a collarless top.

YOU WILL NEED

• a sheet of paper and a pencil • calico (or other scrap fabric of a similar weight to your fabric) • fabric for collar • tailor's chalk • scissors • sewing machine • thread in matching colour • trim or bias binding • iron • press-studs

HOW TO

1. Draw your collar to the desired shape, size and design on the paper

2. Use your drawing to create a toile (mock-up) of the Peter Pan collar out of your calico/scrap fabric

3. Tweak the toile until you get the desired size and shape

4. Find the midpoint of the dress and the toile

5. Match up the 2 midpoints and chalk the shape of the collar onto the pre-existing collar or your new fabric

6. Cut out the new collar shape

7. Zigzag-sew the raw edge (see 'Stop fraying')

8. Hand-sew trim or bias binding around collar edge

9. Press with an iron to finish

10. If your collar isn't already attached to your garment, sew 3 small press studs onto the collar: 1 at the midpoint and 1 at each end

11. Mark with chalk the positions of the press studs on the garment, and sew on

HINT

To get a symmetrical collar, double up your fabric before drawing the half-shape on and cutting it out

WORK WITH LEATHER

Leather is not only very hard-wearing, but also can look great added as a trim to pocket edges. Bear the following points in mind to work successfully with leather as you would any other fabric.

1. Lamb's leather is softer and easier to work with than cow's leather

2. Use a leather needle on your sewing machine. They have a chisel-point so they can cut as they sew.

3. Cut straight lines in leather using a scalpel running against a metal ruler.

4. Regular pins aren't strong enough to go through leather, so use double-sided sticky tape to hold it in place for sewing instead

CREATE PUFFED SLEEVES

YOU WILL NEED

• stitch unpicker • sewing machine • matching thread • pins • tape measure • tailor's chalk

HOW TO

1. Unpick the sleeve just at the sleeve head area, leaving it attached at the underarm

2. With the machine set to its longest straight stich, sew 2 parallel lines 5mm apart, close to the sleeve-top edge. Back tack at one end, but allow the threads to run free at the other end.

3. Carefully pull the 2 top threads at the loose end of the stitches to 'gather' the fabric along the sewn lines until you have created gathers in the sleeve

4. Ease the gathers evenly across the stitches with your fingers and pin sleeve back to the arm hole

5. Check this smaller arm hole still fits your arms

6. Measure the new circumference of the arm hole

7. Turn the garment inside out with right sides together, shoulder seam at top

8. Taper the shoulder seam to desired circumference by gathering excess fabric along the shoulder in dart shape, and pin

9. Mark new shoulder seam line in chalk

10. Machine sew the new shoulder seam

11. Rejoin the sleeve and the arm hole, pinning in place with right sides of fabric together

12. Machine sew together along original stitch marks

Secured stitches

Loose stitches (2)

 ## FRESHEN UP VELVET

You can try these tips on tired velvet.

1. Use an iron with a steaming function, but don't let the hot iron touch the velvet or it will mark it

2. Use the steam from a boiling kettle on the wrong side of the fabric and then brush the right side with a dry clothes brush

I buy most of my vintage online. It can seem overwhelming, but just think of the choice out there. Hundreds and hundreds of brilliant vintage shops, and then millions of people selling their things on eBay and Etsy. It's where all of the best pieces are for the best prices, so you should give it a go.

If you want to find something designer then go to the list of designers on pages 108–109 and look them up to see whose styles you like and what is for sale. If it's Zandra Rhodes, for example, simply type into your search engine 'vintage Zandra Rhodes', and see where it takes you. That is how I do it. It's so easy. So easy that I think I just patronised you quite dramatically. If I did, sorry. If I didn't, where the hell have you been?

To be more specific, type exactly what you are looking for into eBay. Try it now. Type: 'vintage red dress' and then your size. Press search. See? Now you see a load of vintage red dresses. Keep scrolling through them. It might feel like it's taking ages, but imagine how long it would have taken to go into a shop.

Always read the description fully

Be careful of items that are listed as 'vintage style', as they are most probably reproductions. Sellers on eBay are pretty good at listing all of the details of the item and what era it is from. They will also list any damage or condition issues, and if you are unsure then always ask the seller for more information if you need it. And be sure to check postage and package prices, as that can bump up the cost a bit if it isn't local.

Know your measurements

This is the best way to not be disappointed, although don't forget you can take anything to a tailor. So if the clothes measurements are a little too small, ask the seller if there is any seam allowance. And if it's too big or too long, then buy it and get it taken in or up.

The easiest way to measure yourself is to take several pieces of your favourite clothing – the pieces that fit you the best – and measure them. Measure them lying flat, then double the measurements for all of these areas:

Shoulder to shoulder • Bust • Waist • Hips • Inseam • Shoulder to waist • Waist to crotch • Thigh width (if you plan to buy trousers) • Armhole (for plus size)

That should be all you need to find yourself some bargains online. Just get involved – you will soon work it out.

If eBay or Etsy freak you out because there is just too much, check out some of my favourite sites listed at the end of the book. Like shops, these gorgeous sites have done brilliant edits of their stock so you can take your pick from all the beauties they have on sale.

If I don't get to them first, that is.

Here are some great tips on how to keep your vintage in tip-top condition. If you are ever unsure if a fabric can take it or not, then wait and ask an expert. Remember, these clothes are old and sometimes very delicate; just use your head, and, again, don't blame me if it all goes wrong.

GET RID OF BO FROM UNWASHABLE CLOTHES

Put cheap vodka in a spray bottle and spray the armpits. Dilute it depending on the delicacy of the fabric. Let it air dry – do not put any heat near it.

GET RID OF YELLOW STAINS

Mix vodka with equal parts of water and soak the fabric in it to get rid of yellow stains on washables.

OR

Crush a couple of aspirin in a cup of water and rub it into the stain. Leave for fifteen minutes and wash off. Repeat as needed.

KEEP CREASES IN TROUSERS

Gently run a bar of soap along the trouser crease line and then press with an iron. Make sure no one is wearing the trousers as you do this.

MAKE A STUBBORN ZIP RUN SMOOTHLY

Rub a candle along the teeth. The zip's teeth, not your teeth. Just to be clear.

GET RID OF YELLOWING OR AGE STAINS FROM WHITE CLOTHES

Soak in a wool softener or nappy solution, hang out or lie flat in the sunshine, but don't rinse. When dry, rinse well and lay out flat on a towel to dry, inside or in the shade.

If all else fails, use dress shields. They are weird plastic flaps that look a bit like sanitary towels. They go in your armpits. It's how they used to deal with sweaties. Actually, you know what? Don't. They are hideous. Get a different dress.

KEEP CLOTHES SMELLING FRESH

Never use so-called fabric freshener sprays. They are synthetic and toxic. They don't mask smells – they enhance them. Use natural fresheners such as lavender, cedar, mint or rosemary sprigs. Hang them in your wardrobe – but not touching the garments in case they stain.

Nothing beats the smell of fresh clothes that have hung outside for a few hours. Do this several times a year to avoid mustiness.

HANG YOUR CLOTHES

Use those pretty padded hangers. Never use wire hangers – they are a garment's worst friend. It's the clothing equivalent of sitting on a really uncomfortable chair that hurts your bum. Don't put your frocks through it.

AVOID MOTH HOLES

Use cedar wood or lavender to keep moths away. They smell much nicer than mothballs.

If possible, put clothes in a pillowcase and put in a chest freezer for a few hours to kill any bugs. This goes for any clothes with moth holes. Washing doesn't kill them. Freeze the crap out of the little sods. Remove all stains from clothing before putting them in the wardrobe – apparently moths find them delicious. Mmm, stale wine!

STORE NATURAL FABRICS

Hang in the dark – sunlight ruins natural fabrics.

STORE BIAS-CUT DRESSES

Never hang up a bias-cut dress as it will stretch and become out of shape. Wrap in acid-free tissue and store folded up.

CLEAN KID-LEATHER GLOVES

Put them on your hands and wash with glycerine soap, rinsing well. Dry your hands/gloves with a towel and leave the gloves to dry flat, with no heat. Put them back on when dry to soften them up again.

GET RID OF OIL ON A DRESS

Dab a small (read: tiny) amount of eucalyptus or tea tree oil on the oil before washing, either by hand or machine. It also makes it smell nice!

WASH FRAGILE GARMENTS

Hand-wash – never be tempted to put in the machine.

MAKE YOUR OWN SUIT/GARMENT BAGS

Use calico or a nice printed cotton – or even an old sheet. Cut two oblongs big enough to fit the clothes in, sew around two long sides and one narrow edge. Make a large hem on the unsewn edge, leaving a gap to thread a drawstring through.

STORE WOOL

Woollen garments are best stored flat as they can distort over time when hung up.

STOP RUNS IN STOCKINGS OR TIGHTS

Dab clear nail varnish at the top and bottom of the ladder.

REMOVE CREASES ON DELICATE ITEMS

Hang garments in the bathroom when you run a bath or shower. The steam helps remove creases. But don't do what I do and come out of the shower and think the dress is a human and almost have a heart attack. Never a good look when naked. Alternatively, get a steamer.

Double lucky

I love this dress so much. It's really stiff, bold and flattering. I love the colours and the geometry. I love the length and how the waist looks dropped because of the red line, but it is actually really nicely defined by a seam about five inches above it. I fell in love with this dress at first sight, and didn't question the £200 price tag. I bought it to wear to Wimbledon, because it looked sporty but also very structured.

Then, while on my vintage travels, I stumbled across this second dress. I couldn't believe my luck: one of my fave dresses in another colour. This hardly ever happens with vintage. But when I looked closer, I whooped louder. This dress was fully lined and labelled. Little had I known that the first one was a Louis Féraud. Absolutely worth the £200 I paid for it, if not more. But – and this is where you will see how vintage pricing is often just a seller's choice – the new one cost just £45. The fully lined and labelled one was £155 cheaper than my original purchase. I obviously bought it and will probably wear the new one to Wimbledon next year. I still don't regret the £200; in honesty, I think the person selling the one for £45 made a massive boo-boo. (Does anyone say boo-boo any more?)

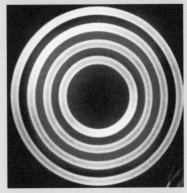

Aunty's treasure

Remember how I said you will be searching everywhere to find hidden gems? Well, look no further than your mum's and aunties' wardrobes. I found this Ossie Clark beauty in my Aunty Jane's wardrobe a few years ago. It's the kind of dress that is so rare you'd be lucky to ever find anything like it in a shop. I love Ossie Clark and I trawl for his pieces, but I've never seen anything quite like this. It's a very heavy cotton shirt dress with cute ruffled sleeves and a big lapel. Screamingly 70s and really nicely fitted. It looks like the print is painted on, and it's a Celia Birtwell design, so it needs very careful and professional cleaning, but it's pretty hard-wearing and I get so much use out of it.

My aunt bought it in Guernsey in the late 70s and only wore it twice, so it's in perfect condition. Who knew this had been up in my aunty's bedroom all that time? I could have been a much more stylish teenager if I had known. Mind you, I am not sure something like this would have worked in the 90s, seeing as that genuinely was the decade that fashion forgot . . . or at least should forget. And yeah, it's me saying that.

And no, I don't think I will feel differently in thirty years' time. I look back at photos of me as a teenager and want to hide them under a rock. I'm sorry to everyone who came into contact with me. I didn't mean to be so offensive with my outfit choices.

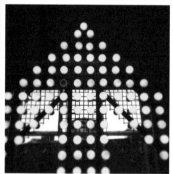

Best ever jumpsuit

This jumpsuit drives me wild. The colour is unreal – jade, I think? But such a brilliant shade of green, really unusual. And I love the utilitarian look of the suit – it's so obviously 70s, but the wide leg and worker vibe hints back to the 40s, like the 70s so often did. This is so comfortable, and long in the body. Which is always a good thing, because nobody wants a camel toe. I love how thick the straps are so that wearing a bra is no problem, and the material is rayon, so very easy to care for. But the thing I love most about this jumpsuit is that it cost £26. Good work, Beyond Retro!

Pucci Pucci poo

I am crazy about this skirt. It's a vintage Pucci velvet maxi skirt. It's fully lined and really long, with only a few teeny marks on it. I got it from a website called Lovely's Vintage Emporium, which sells some really fun things. This one cost £249, which I know isn't cheap. But if you walk into a Pucci store, you will see that, comparatively, it's a pretty good deal. But Pucci or not, I still think I would have bought it. It's perfect in the winter with an Arran jumper and brown leather boots. I wear it with a brown cape and a floppy hat. It's possibly my favourite item of winter vintage, and I've never seen anyone in anything like it. Pucci is such a fun brand, but I definitely prefer their vintage to their more modern stuff. And here is a little bit of trivia for you: Marilyn Monroe was buried in a Pucci dress. I might just get buried in a velvet Pucci skirt one day.

Wedding dress, anyone?

I saw this dress in Scarlet Vintage in Bath. It was on a mannequin and I couldn't take my eyes off it. Unfortunately, I was shopping for somebody else, and she saw it before I did and wanted to try it on. I remember being torn. I wanted her to find something she loved, but I wanted this dress so much. Anyway . . . luckily for me, she loved it but it wasn't right on her. So I called the shop later and asked them to put it aside; this dress was not to be the one that got away.

I love how delicate it is, and the condition is spectacular. So spectacular I had to question its age. I mean, it looks 20s but can't be. And no, it isn't. The lady in the shop told me that it had been brought in the day before by a woman who bought it from Harrods in the 70s. She had never worn it. There had been a 20s revival in the 70s when the first *Great Gatsby* film came out, so you find a lot of 70s flapper dresses. I now know to be slightly suspicious of 20s dresses in immaculate condition, as they could have the same story as this one. Anyway, it's gorgeous and now it's mine, so gerroff! Unless you genuinely want to get married in it, and then I will happily lend it to you. I'm very, very serious. *awaits tweet*

BEFORE YOU GO . . .

Some people say they don't care about fashion, but what they don't realise is that they are as defined by what they wear as the people who do. The clothes you wear create an image of you that people will remember – not just now, but after you have gone. One day, those who love you will look to photos of you to complete their memories. Imagine yourself in that photo in the clothes you are wearing today. Will what you have on remind them how fun you were? How kind? How smart? How creative? If not, then maybe it's time to match who you really are with the clothes that you wear. And I reckon you've got more chance of getting it right with vintage than you do on the high street.

I think you've got the message. Tweet me the pictures of your discoveries. I will be waiting to get to know you from the clothes that you choose.

Enjoy the rummaging.

Dawn x
@hotpatooties

BATH

Scarlet Vintage
5 Queen Street
Bath BA1 1HE
www.scarletvintage.co.uk

We do our buying wherever we can find good-quality, unusual pieces. We travel to the US frequently, particularly New York and California. We love the US because of the range available. Because they never had rationing like in the UK, the 40s and 50s clothes tend to be better fabrics and brighter colours.

The 50s are perennially popular with our clients. The dresses are not so old and delicate that you worry about wearing them (unlike those from the 20s and 30s) and they are super-feminine – perfect for a special occasion if you want to feel great.

Vintage to Vogue
28 Milsom Street
Bath BA1 1DG
www.vintagetovoguebath.co.uk

BIRMINGHAM

Cow
82–85 Digbeth High Street
Birmingham B5 6DY
www.wearecow.com

Gingermegs
Unit 6
The Terraces
Gibb Street
Custard Factory
Birmingham B9 4AA
www.gingermegs-vintage.com

BLACKBURN

Decades
20 Lord Street West
Blackburn
Lancashire BB2 1JX
www.decadesvintagefashion.jimdo.com

BOURNEMOUTH

What Alice Found
805 Christchurch Road
Boscombe
Dorset BH7 6AP
www.whatalicefound.co.uk/vintageboutique

BRIGHTON

Bobby and Dandy
18 Blatchington Road
Hove
East Sussex BN3 3YN
www.bobbyanddandy.co.uk

Dirty Harry,
6 Sydney Street,
Brighton
BN1 4EN
www.dirtyharryltd.com

Hope & Harlequin
31 Sydney Street
Brighton BN1 4EP
www.hopeandharlequin.com

To Be Worn Again
12 Kensington Gardens
Brighton
East Sussex BN1 4AL

24 Sydney Street
Brighton
East Sussex BN1 4EN
www.tobewornagain.co.uk

Tramp
22 Trafalgar Street
Brighton
BN1 4EQ
www.trampvintageclothing.com

Vanstone
51 Upper North Street
Brighton
East Sussex BN1 3FH

Wolf & Gypsy Vintage
30 Sydney Street
North Laine
Brighton BN1 4EP
www.wolfandgypsyvintage.co.uk

BRISTOL

The Birdcage
28 Clare Street
Bristol BS1 1YE
www.birdcagebristol.com

Clifton Vintage Boutique
Clifton Arcade
5 Clifton Arcade
Bristol
BS8 4AA
www.cliftonarcade.co.uk

Urban Fox
58 Corn Street
Bristol BS1 1JG
www.urbanfox.me

DUBLIN

Jenny Vander
50 Drury Street
Dublin
Ireland

The 3rd Policeman
121 Lower Rathmines Road
Dublin 6
Ireland
www.the3rdpoliceman.com

The Harlequin
13 Castle Market
Dublin 2
Ireland
www.theharlequinvintage.com

EDINBURGH

Herman Brown
No. 151 West Port
Edinburgh EH3 9DP
www.hermanbrown.co.uk

The Frayed Hem
45 Cockburn Street
Edinburgh EH1 1BS
www.thefrayedhem.com

Those Were the Days
26 St Stephen Street
Stockbridge
Edinburgh EH3 5AL
www.thosewerethedaysvintage.com/index.html

W. Armstrong & Son
83 The Grassmarket
Edinburgh EH1 2HJ

64–66 Clerk Street
Edinburgh EH8 9JB

14 Teviot Place
Edinburgh EH1 2QZ
www.armstrongsvintage.co.uk

ESSEX

Boutique Unique
91 Broadway West
Leigh-on-Sea
Essex SS9 2BU
www.boutique-b-u.co.uk/store

Those who have never bought vintage before are always a bit hesitant at first, but after seeing the quality and how unique the garment is, they are quickly turned – especially once they see the price!

EXETER

The Real McCoy
21 McCoys Arcade
Fore Street
Exeter
Devon EX4 3AN
www.therealmccoy.co.uk

GLASGOW

Mr Ben
Kings Court
101 King Street
Glasgow G1 2RB
www.mrbenretroclothing.com

HARROGATE

Catherine Smith Vintage
57a Cold Bath Road
Harrogate HG2 0NL
www.catherinesmithvintage.co.uk

KENT

Love Is Boutique
Romary House
26 Church Road
Tunbridge Wells
Kent TN1 1JP
www.loveisboutique.co.uk

LEEDS

Blue Rinse
9–11 Call Lane
Leeds
West Yorkshire LS1 7DH
www.bluerinsevintage.co.uk

Mad Elizabeth Vintage
Leeds Corn Exchange
Call Lane
Leeds LS1 7BR
www.madelizabeth.co.uk

Pop Boutique
12–16 Central Road
Leeds LS1 6DE
www.pop-boutique.com

UpStaged Vintage
No.1 White Cloth Hall
Crown Street
Leeds LS2 7DA
www.upstagedleeds.co.uk

> I'm too fickle to pick a favourite era. But we are privileged to look back at the twentieth century from right here: to dress up for 40s weekenders without fear of air-raids; to feel and buy 'revolutionary' new fabrics from the 50s without a ration book – and we can take digital photos of ourselves wearing them. However attractive an Art Deco telephone is, if my car breaks down on the motorway I'm bloody glad to have my mobile phone.

LINCOLN

Tasty Vintage
9 Steep Hill
Lincoln LN2 1LT
www.tastyvintage.com

LIVERPOOL

69A
75 Renshaw Street
Liverpool L1 2SJ
www.69aliverpool.co.uk

Deep
91 Bold Street
Liverpool L1 1HF
www.deepvintageclothing.co.uk

Pop Boutique
58 Whitechapel
Liverpool L1 6EG
www.pop-boutique.com

Quiggins Attique
325 Aigburth Road
Liverpool
Merseyside L17 0BL
www.quigginsattique.
blogspot.co.uk

Raiders Vintage
38 Renshaw Street
Liverpool L1 4EF
www.facebook.com/
raidersvintage

LONDON

Absolute Vintage
15 Hanbury Street
London E1 6QR
www.absolutevintage.co.uk

> The most exciting item we ever had was probably the ridiculously heavily beaded white bustier gown that was used for the final UK performance of *Billy Elliot*.

Alfie's Antiques
13–25 Church Street
Marylebone
London
NW8 8DT
www.alfiesantiques.com

Annie's Antiques
12 Camden Passage
London
N1 8ED
www.anniesvintageclothing.co.uk

Bang Bang
9 Berwick Street
London
W1F 0PJ

21 Goodge Street
London
W1T 2PJ
www.bangbangclothingexchange.co.uk

Beyond Retro
58-59 Great Marlborough
    Street
London W1F 7JY

110–112 Cheshire Street
London E2 6EJ

92–100 Stoke Newington
    Road
London N16 7XB
www.beyondretro.com

Blitz
55–59 Hanbury Street
London E1 5JP
www.blitzlondon.co.uk

Blondie
Unit 2
114–118 Commercial Street
London E1 6NF
www.blondievintage.co.uk

Deborah Woolf
28 Church Street
London
NW8 8EP
www.deborahwoolf.com

Gillian Horsup
1-7 Davies Mews
London
W1K 5AB
www.gillianhorsup.com

Hirst Antiques
59 Pembridge Road
London W11 3HN
www.hirstantiques.co.uk

House of Vintage
4 Cheshire Street
London E2 6EH
www.houseofvintageuk.com

Hunky Dory Vintage
226 Brick Lane
London
E1 6SA
www.hunkydoryvintage.com

Insight
201 Munster Road
London SW6 6BX

Lucy in Disguise
48 Lexington Street
London W1F 0LR
www.lucyindisguiselondon.com

Merchant Archive
19 Kensington Park Road
London
W11 2EU
www.merchantarchive.com

Miniola
65 Cross Street
Islington
London N1 2BB
www.miniola.co.uk

Mint Vintage
71–73 Stoke Newington
  High Street
London N16 8EL
www.mintvintage.co.uk

Mishka
210–212 Middle Lane
London N8 7LA

One of a Kind
259 Portobello Road
Notting Hill
London W11 1LR
www.oneofakindvintagestore.com

Orsini
76 Earls Court Road
Kensington
W8 6EQ
www.orsinivintage.co.uk

Painted Black
22 Veryan Court
Crouch End
London
N8 8JR
www.paintedblack.co.uk

Paper Dress Vintage
114–116 Curtain Road
London EC2A 3AH
www.paperdressvintage.co.uk

Peekaboo
2 Ganton Street
London
W1F 7QL
www.peekaboovintage.com

Pop Boutique
6 Monmouth Street
London WC2 9HB
www.pop-boutique.com

Radio Days
7 Lower Marsh
London SE1 7AB
www.radiodaysvintage.co.uk

Reign Wear
12 Berwick Street
London W1F 0PN

Rellik
8 Golborne Road
London W10 5NW
www.relliklondon.co.uk

Revival Retro
2.11 Kingly Court
London
W1B 5PW
www.revival-retro.com

Rokit
101 & 107 Brick Lane
London E1 6SE

225 High Street
London NW1 7BU

42 Shelton Street
London WC2H 9HZ
www.rokit.co.uk

Scarlet Rage Vintage
11 Topsfield Road
Crouch End
London N8 8DT
www.scarletragevintage.com

Spitalfields Market
Brushfield Street
Spitalfields
London E1 6AA
www.spitalfields.co.uk

The Vintage Showroom
14 Earlham Street
London WC2H 9LN
www.thevintageshowroom.com

Vien
87 Church Road
Crystal Palace
London
SE19 2TA
www.vienvintage.co.uk

Vintage Modes
1–7 Davies Mews
London W1K 5AB
www.vintagemodes.co.uk

MANCHESTER

Cow
Unit C1
City Tower
Parker Street
Piccadilly Gardens
Manchester M1 4AH
www.wearecow.com

Deep
10 Hilton Street
Manchester M1 1JF
www.deepvintageclothing.co.uk

Pop Boutique
34–36 Oldham Street
Manchester M1 1JN
www.pop-boutique.com

Retro Rehab
91 Oldham Street
Manchester M4 1LW
www.facebook.com/pages/Retro-rehab-Manchester/446652315110

MARLBOROUGH

Foxtrot Vintage
2 High Street
Marlborough SN8 1AA
www.foxtrot-vintage-clothing.com

MIDDLESBROUGH

Deep
153 Linthorpe Road
Middlesbrough TS1 4AG
www.deepvintageclothing.co.uk

NEWCASTLE

Attica Vintage
2 Old George Yard
High Bridge
Newcastle upon Tyne
NE1 1EZ
www.atticavintage.co.uk

Deep
51 Highbridge
Newcastle upon Tyne
NE1 1AW
www.deepvintageclothing.co.uk

NORWICH

Goldfinches
4 St Gregorys Alley
Norwich NR2 1ER
www.goldfinchesvintage.co.uk

Prim
14 St Benedicts Street
Norwich
Norfolk
NR2 4AG
www.primvintagefashion.com

Retreat Vintage
26a Magdalen Street
Norwich NR3 1HU
www.retreatvintage.co.uk

NOTTINGHAM

Celia's
80 Derby Road
Nottingham NG1 5FD
www.celias-nottm.co.uk/shop

Cow
3 Carlton Street
Hockley
Nottingham NG1 1NL
www.wearecow.com

OXFORD

Reignwear
136 Cowley Road
Oxford
OX4 1JE

READING

Alexandra Vintage
42 Market Place
Reading
Berkshire RG1 2DE
www.alexandravintage.com

> The 40s would be my favourite era, for its stripped-back utility fashion – how with such little material such style was achieved.

Frock n Roll
11 Watlington Street
Reading
Berks
RG14 4RQ
www.frockandroll.com

SALISBURY

Foxtrot Vintage
47 Fisherton Street
Town Centre
Salisbury SP2 7SU
www.foxtrot-vintage-clothing.com

SHEFFIELD

Bang Bang Vintage
19 Westfield Terrace
Sheffield
South Yorkshire S1 4GH
www.bangbangvintage.com

Cow
156–160 West Street
Sheffield S1 4ES
www.wearecow.com

Freshmans
6–8 Carver Street
Sheffield S1 4FS
www.freshmans.co.uk

SOMERSET

Lark Vintage
20 Paul Street
Frome
Somerset BA11 1DT
www.larkvintage.co.uk

Donna May Vintage
28 Catherine Hill
Frome
Somerset BA11 1BY
www.donnamayvintage.com

SUFFOLK

Vintage Angels
Hall Farm
Aldeburgh
Suffolk IP15 5JD
www.vintageangelsclothing.co.uk

YORK

Deep
26 Fossgate
York YO1 9TA
www.deepvintageclothing.co.uk

Priestleys
11 Grape Lane
York YO1 7HU

We chose our name because 'Priestleys' was written into the tiles of the shop we started in, an old Victorian butcher's shop.

Chloë Sevigny happened upon us when she was in town to see Morrissey and snapped up a pair of patchwork denim jeans and a fabulous Gaultier corset top that could have been made for her.

Purple Haze
52 Fossgate
York YO1 9TF
www.purplehazevintage.com

Modern fashion is designed not to last, which is different from vintage clothing, which was made extremely well and repaired and darned.

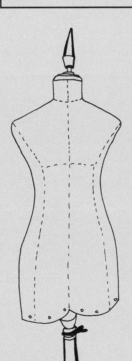

ONLINE

Atelier Mayer
www.atelier-mayer.com

Betty Rae
www.bettyraevintage.com

Black Cat Boutique
www.theblackcatboutique.co.uk

Devoted 2 Vintage
www.devoted2vintage.co.uk

Gillian Horsup
www.gillianhorsup.com

It's Vintage Darling
www.itsvintagedarling.com

Jannes Vintage
www.jannesvintage.com

Judy's Affordable Vintage Fair
www.judysvintagefair.co.uk

Juno Says Hello
www.junosayshello.com

Lou Lou's Vintage Fair
www.thevintagefair.com

Love Miss Daisy
www.lovemissdaisy.com

Lovely's Vintage Emporium
www.lovelys-vintage-emporium.myshopify.com

Mad Elizabeth Vintage
www.madelizabeth.co.uk

My Vintage
www.myvintage.co.uk

Natasha Bailie
www.natashabailie.com

Peekaboo Vintage
www.peekaboovintage.com

Portobello Market
www.portobelloroad.co.uk

Retro Daisy
www.retrodaisy.com

Retro Sun
Retrosun.co.uk

Rock My Vintage
www.rockmyvintage.co.uk

Rokit
www.rokit.co.uk

Susan Caplan
www.susancaplan.co.uk

Tara Starlet
www.tarastarlet.com

The Stellar Boutique
www.thestellarboutique.com

Vintage Deli
www.vintagedeli.co.uk

Virtual Vintage
www.virtualvintageclothing.co.uk

VVV
www.vvvintage.com

William Vintage
www.williamvintage.com

And then my very own,
BOB Vintage
www.bobbydop.com

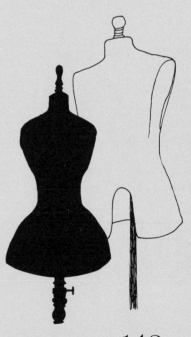

THANK YOU

I want to thank my husband for enduring endless fashion shows, and my friends and sister for letting me dress them up as soon as they walk through the front door.

And thanks to every single shop, website and vintage dealer who gave us access to their stock to make this book, and the TV show, as gorgeous as it could be. Thank you!

Thank you to Jay Hunt and Gill Wilson at C4 for powering on with *This Old Thing*.

And to Jim Allen at RDF Television, and Andrew Anderson and Mike Matthews for working so hard on a series that was a joy to make. Thank you to absolutely every member of the crew of *This Old Thing*, and all our cast and contributors. Thank you William Banks-Blaney for teaching me loads and your wonderful interview and gorgeous moments in the TV show. Thanks to my assistant Buzz for being a trooper and Helen Boyle and the style team for working tirelessly with me on the looks for the show. Thank you to David Loftus for the beautiful photography and Anita Mangan for putting it all together. Thank you to Hot Key Books for doing the book with me – I can't have imagined doing it with anyone else. And Emily Thomas for the support I have become reliant on, and Jenny Jacoby for all the fine tuning and approval of Dawnisms such as 'thigh-brows'.

Thank you to designers past and present who continue to inspire me and to everyone who lets me bang on about old threads.

For Hot Key Books

Publisher: Emily Thomas
Edited and Project Managed by Jenny Jacoby
Designed by Anita Mangan
Illustrations by Anita Mangan
Thanks to Amber Butchart, Holly Kyte, Jennifer Whitehead

For RDF

Andrew Anderson
Photographs by David Loftus

Thank you to our vintage photo contributors . . .

Amy Astley • Bianca Wright • Brenda Morrissey • Caroline Neal • Cheryl Gunning • Chloe Lefroy • Emma Peacock • Emma Wolford • Faye Webster • Harriet Leggatt-Auld • Helen Carey • Jenny Jacoby • Kathleen Nicholls • Kathryn Fielding • Laura Milne • Lizzy Nairn • Melanie Bell • Naomi Colthurst • Sameera Al-Hilley • Sarah Wathen

Photo credits:

Pages 22a, 23, 25, 27a, 28, 30, 31, 33a, b, 34, 35, 37a, b, 38, 40, 41, 42, 43, 45, 46, 48f, 49a, 50c, 51, 52, 53, 54, 55d, 57, 60, 61a, c, 62, 64, 65a, 67, 68a, 70b, 71a, 73b, c, d, 74, 75, 76, 77, 79b, c, 81, 82b, 83, 84, 85, 86, 87, 88, 89, 90, 91a, b, 93a, 94a, b, c, e, 96b, c, © Getty images

Page 26 © WilliamVintage

Pages 63, 67 Egyptian print dress from Black Cat Boutique

Pages 68b, c, d, 96a, 128, 129a, 131 © Hot Key Books

All others © RDF Television
Illustrations © Anita Mangan

First published in Great Britain in 2014 by Hot Key Books, Northburgh House, 10 Northburgh Street, London EC1V 0AT

Copyright © Dawn O'Porter and RDF Television 2014

A CIP catalogue record for this book is available from the British Library.

ISBN: 978-1-4714-0309-5

10 9 8 7 6 5 4 3 2 1

This book is typeset in LinoLetter and Alternate Gothic.
Colour reproduction by Aylesbury Studios Ltd.
Printed and bound by Butler Tanner & Dennis
Hot Key Books supports the Forest Stewardship Council (FSC), the leading international forest certification organisation, and is committed to printing only on Greenpeace-approved FSC-certified paper.

www.hotkeybooks.com

Hot Key Books is part of the Bonnier Publishing Group

www.bonnierpublishing.com

FSC
www.fsc.org
MIX
Paper from responsible sources
FSC® C120494